HOW DID WARREN BUFFETT SUCCEED?

How I Went from Broke to Millionaire in Under Nine Years Following Warren Buffett's Step-By-Step Guide to Stock Market Success

James E. Pierre, JD

STORY MERCHANT BOOKS
LOS ANGELES
2018

STORY MERCHANT BOOKS

ISBN: 978-0-9991621-4-9

Story Merchant Books
400 S. Burnside Avenue #11B
Los Angeles, CA 90036
http://www.storymerchantbooks.com

Cover Design By Claire Moore, www.529books.com,
a Story Merchant Sister Company
Interior Design By IndieDesignz, www.indiedesignz.com

For my mentors

Warren Buffett, Roger Lowenstein, and Phil Town

TABLE OF CONTENTS

INTRODUCTION

WHO THE HELL IS WARREN BUFFETT?

If you don't know who Warren Buffett is, shame on you! Because, believe me when I tell you, he knows who *you* are. Okay, maybe not *personally*. But if you've ever bought a Duracell battery for your TV's remote controller; if you've ever insured your car with Geico; if you've ever put on a pair of Fruit of the Loom underwear; if you've ever topped your burger with some gooey Heinz catsup, or squeezed some Heinz mustard sauce on your hotdog; if you've ever swiped your American Express, Visa, or MasterCard at any vendor's establishment; if you've ever shopped at Costco or Walmart; if you've ever mowed your lawn using a John Deere tractor; if you've ever sprinkled a little Johnson & Johnson's baby powder on yourself (or lathered your skin with their lotion and oil products); if you've ever ordered a package using UPS; if you've ever pumped gas in your car at a Phillips 66 fueling station…

Okay, I think you get the point.

What I'm saying is: If you've ever purchased any of the products or services mentioned above (and chances are you have), your money went into one man's pocket. Warren Buffett.

No way, you say?

Yes way, I say!

But then you ask, *How can* ***one*** *man own* ***all*** *of those companies?*

And that's when I reply with three words: *The Stock Market.*

Warren Buffett is a stock market investor. The greatest stock market investor of all time. How great? Well… If you would have handed Warren Buffett $1,000 in 1964 and told him to invest it for you, you would now have $10.5 million. That's right. Like some wand-waving magician, he would have taken your measly one thousand dollars and turned it into over *ten million dollars* of cold, hard cash!

That's who Warren E. Buffett is.

Now, I'm going to say something, and I need you to listen carefully. Are you paying attention? Good. Here it is: You will be a millionaire nine years from today, *if* you follow the instructions in this book! You wanna know how I know? Because, chances are, if you shoot exactly like LeBron James, you'll score like LeBron James; and if you swim exactly like Michael Phelps, you'll win a lot of gold medals like Michael Phelps; and if you swing a Louisville slugger exactly like Mike Trout (he's a baseball player currently playing for the Los Angeles Angels), you'll hit a lot of home runs like Mike Trout.

So, I'm going to go out on a limb and say that, if you master the exact techniques that the great ones used to achieve their success, chances are you'll be successful too.

And there's no greater stock market investor than Warren Buffett.

So why don't all stock market investors invest like Buffett, so that they can become rich and successful, too? you ask.

Well… because they're stupid.

But, you're not. Stupid, that is. That's why you picked up this book. Because you want to be rich. And you want to be rich by using the best money-multiplier known to man: The Stock Market. And you figured, *Hey, if I'm gonna get rich using the stock market, why not follow in the footprints of the best stock market investor of all time?*

Duh.

Well, that's why I wrote this book. To show you how Warren did it… so that you can do it too!

But there may be a little, pessimistic voice in the back of your mind, whispering unscrupulously in your ears: *But how do you know this technique will* ***really*** *work?*

Okay, well how about this for an answer: Because it freakin' did!

So you can tell that pessimistic voice to shove off, because I, me, *moi*, the author of this book, used the technique I'm about to teach you, in mid-2008, and, *voila*, I became a millionaire by 2013, at the age of 30.

So take it from me. What I am about to show you is as close to an exact science as you can get on the subject of maximizing your stock market success.

But before I formally introduce myself, let me tell you a little bit more about Warren Buffett, primarily because his background—like his many accomplishments —are an inspiration for this book.

How Did Warren Buffett Succeed?

Many people think that only those who are born into money can really achieve large-scale wealth. That's not necessarily true. While it takes money to make money (and don't ever listen to anyone who tells you differently), you don't have to inherit money in order to become wealthy. Out of the 585 billionaires currently residing in the United States, 62% (or 363 of them) are self-made[1]. Which means that a majority of all the corporate tycoons in this country started with nothing, and, using self-discipline, hard work, and astute money-management skills, they became titans of wealth.

Warren Buffett is no different.

Warren Edward Buffett—self-made, stock market billionaire—was born on August 30, 1930. Now, if you know anything about this country's financial history, the year 1930 should ring a bell. 1930 was the beginning of the Great Depression. The Great Depression was the largest economic catastrophe the United States ever experienced. The depression lasted about ten years, wiped out 50% of the country's banks, leveled 54% of the country's entire economic output, and left over 15 million people unemployed (which equated to 30% of the workforce, and about 12% of the overall population, at the time)[2].

[1] https://www.entrepreneur.com/article/269593

[2] http://www.cbwealthadvisory.com/greatdepression.php

Yep. This is the shit-storm Warren Buffett was born into.

Both of his parents—like the remainder of the population—were unemployed and broke. In fact, Warren Buffett's father, Howard Buffett, was a stockbroker working for Union Street Bank at the time. And one summer afternoon—on August 13, 1931 to be exact—Howard returned from work with some bad news: His employer, Union Street Bank, had shuts its doors, and he—Howard Buffett, the family's sole bread-winner—was out of a job. But the bad news didn't end there. No sir. Because not only was Howard's salary gone, so too was the entire family's savings nest. So, in essence, the Buffett's had zilch. Nada. $0 to their name.

And this all happened 17 days before Warren Buffett's first birthday.

Bummer.

Well, to you and me it might seem that way.

But not to Warren E. Buffett. Unh-unh.

The little chubby, blonde-haired boy with the quiet demeanor and deep, penetrating gaze, resolved to be rich, no matter how shitty a hand he'd been dealt. So at age six he bought Juicy Fruit gum packs and six-packs of Coke wholesale, and went door to door selling them at retail prices, happily pocketing the profits. He invested those profits in the stock market at age 11, and turned that investment into more profitable gains.

But Warren didn't stop there. Unh-unh.

Money was Warren's religion. And money is the gateway to independence and freedom in a world where time is mankind's most valuable resource. So, Warren didn't waste either: time, nor money. He structured his daily schedule, concentrating almost every waking hour on activities and business ventures that could earn him a buck. And once that buck was earned, he saved it, then invested it, in order to multiply it.

Although a consummate entrepreneur, Warren did not shy away from the drudgeries of a 9 to 5 job. In fact, he took on two jobs. Two newspaper routes. He worked these two routes—for the *Washington Post*, and the *Times-Herald*—with passionate zeal and attentiveness to detail. And he made lots of money doing it, too. In 1944, at the tender age of 13, Warren was raking in $175 a month, which is equivalent to $2,200 per month in today's money.

And he saved every goddamn penny.

The following year, in 1945, he took what would be equivalent to $15,500 in today's money, from his savings, and invested it in a 40-acre farmland. He rented the farmland to a rancher, who paid him a monthly rental.

But Warren didn't stop there. Unh-unh.

At age 17, he teamed up with a pal, Donald Danly. The two bought a pinball machine for $250 (in today's money). Afterwards, they put the pinball machine in a barbershop not too far from where they lived, and split the machine's earnings with the barbershop's owner. By the end of the first day, they found $150 (in today's money) inside of the machine. Before long, they were earning over $550 (in today's money) every week from seven machines. Donald Danly was a very good handyman and took care of all of the machinery repairs. Warren Buffett, a math whiz even then, was the accountant. They formed a company called Wilson Coin Operated Machines. Then they sold the company the following year for over $16,000 (in today's money). That's a whopping 6,400% return.

In a single, fucking year.

And when Warren was not working, or entrepreneuring (I know, I just made up a word), he was *reading*. Reading every book on business and investing he could get his hands on. So not only was he stacking some serious coin, he was also building his knowledge-base, fine-tuning his financial virtuosity. Thus, by the age of 19, Warren had saved over $98,000 (in today's money) in cold, hard cash from his newspaper routes and business ventures, and had also read over 200 books on business and investing.

And… the rest is history.

Warren would eventually use the stock market to turn his $98,000 savings nest, first, into $1 million (adjusted for inflation), in the span of 6 short years (from 1950-1956). And then, using the same stock market principles, he would later turn that $1 million into what at present is a $75 billion fortune.

Well, I'll be damned, you might be thinking. *How exactly did he do that?*

Well, that's what I'm going to discuss at length in this book. And, hopefully, by the time you're done reading this volume, you'll be able to save and invest your way to retirement in the next nine years, or less.

Just like Warren Buffet did.

And just like I did.

But before we crack open the golden egg, let me tell you a little bit about myself.

Who The Hell Is James Pierre?

If you don't know who James Pierre is, shame on you!

Just kidding.

I'm a nobody, really. But a rich nobody. And I want you to be a rich nobody (or somebody, depending on how you view things), too. If I was able to accumulate $1 million dollars in under nine years, you can too.

I was born on June 22, 1983, in a ghetto in Brooklyn, New York. My parents are Haitian immigrants. At the time, my father was a struggling reverend, and my mom used to hand out promotional flyers on the street for money.

Safe to say, we were broke and had nothing.

Then my mom gave birth to my little sister and brother. So, if we were broke before, now, with *five* mouths to feed and no sustainable income, we became even broker (I think I just made up another word; I tend to do that from time to time, so sue me. Well, don't really sue me. Anyway, I digress).

There is a quote that says: *Poverty is the parent of crime.* Well, hell if that isn't true. Everyone in my neighborhood growing up was poor. So crime ran amuck. The impetus for economic progress in my "hood" revolved around muggings, stabbings, shootings, robberies, and drug dealing. So, sad to say, if you weren't doing any one of these things, chances are you weren't making any loot. At least not any *real* loot.

Now, my family lived in a basement, five bodies crammed into a single room. My parents rented this basement room from my aunt for $500 a month. One day, at the age of 10, I took a good long look at my surroundings and decided, *you know what? The hell with this. Being poor sucks. I wanna be rich*!

So I tried to get rich as fast as possible. I'd skip class to go be a lookout for the neighborhood drug dealers. And although, at times, I made more money in a week than my teachers made in a month, for me, personally, the money wasn't coming in fast enough (especially since I was risking my life and freedom on a daily basis being in the same vicinity as crack-dealing gangsters).

So I took on another profession. It was a trade I'd learned from simply growing up in a fucked up neighborhood.

My new occupation: stealing.

Back then, there was a hand-held gaming device manufactured by Nintendo, called Gameboy. It was all the craze. Every kid who could afford to have one had one. Kids would bring their Gameboys (and Gameboy cartridges) with them everywhere. Including school.

Except, at my school (Public School 198), as well as the surrounding elementary schools and high schools in the neighborhood, Gameboys weren't allowed on faculty premises. So, when a teacher caught you playing your Gameboy on school grounds, he/she would take the Gameboy away from you and lock it away in their desk. The Gameboy would not be returned to you until your parents (or a guardian) actually came to the school to pick it up themselves.

Ding!

The lightbulb went off in my head.

Dollar signs flashed in my eyes, and my mouth watered greedily.

I figured, if I could steal the Gameboys from the teachers' desks (before they could be reclaimed by the parents) I could fence the stolen Gameboys (and Gameboy cartridges) on the street, or sell it back to the stores, for at least half the market value (which at the time was around $75). Either way, it would be all profit for me.

So, I began breaking into teachers' desks after school. And before I knew it, I'd swiped ten Gameboys (and various game cartridges) in a single month and made over $450 reselling them. But, being the overzealous entrepreneur, I wanted to scale my new "business." So, I visited all of the nearby elementary schools and high schools in my neighborhood, and put together a team of thieves, each team consisting of kids that attended those respective schools. I taught them how to break into the teachers' locked desks, in order to steal the Gameboys and cartridges. And before I knew it, I had about 7 teams, stealing about 8 Gameboys each a week. This went on for about 4 months. All told, the entire [criminal] enterprise grossed around $33,000. After "expenses" I netted about $12,000, averaging about $3,000 in passive income per month. Life was good.

And then it wasn't.

Because I got caught (of course).

And expelled from school.

Well, *almost* expelled.

My parents went before the school board and literally cried their eyes out, begging the school administrators to rescind my dismissal. The board eventually did, and I was allowed to come back to school, on the condition that I return any and all Gameboys I currently had in my possession, as well as any proceeds from the sale of the Gameboys I'd already sold.

I learned a valuable lesson that day: *Crime doesn't pay, not really; not in the end.*

So it was back to the drawing board. I thought to myself, *How can I make lots of money without stealing, or drug-dealing, or breaking the law*? The answer came to me at the age of 12. I was a voracious reader, even back then. And one day, while scouring the shelves of my local library, I came across a book. The title was *Buffett: The Making of an American Capitalist*, by Roger Lowenstein.

The man on the cover (Warren Buffett) stood authoritatively, arms crossed over his chest, staring at the reader with a golden twinkle in his eye, and a tiny, knowing smile on his lips. This man, Warren Buffett, *looked* rich. And mightily independent. All of the things *I* wanted to be.

So, I read the book. Actually, I devoured it, finishing the 475-page volume in a single week.

And all of a sudden, I had discovered my destiny.

I'd found my *true* calling.

And that calling was... stock market investing.

Except, not just *any* kind of stock market investing. (Because, trust me, there were lots of investment theories being implemented by scores of investors, both institutional and individual).

The investment strategy that was highlighted in Lowenstein's biography about Warren Buffett was an approach called *value* investing. The book you now hold in your hands will teach you, in large part, the fundamentals of value investing, so that you can apply its methods to your own stock portfolio, in order to maximize your investment returns.

But as intelligent and industrious as Warren Buffett was, he was not the founder of this sure-fire approach. In fact, Warren learned value investing from a man named Benjamin Graham. Ben Graham was a financial professor at Columbia University, from 1928-1955[3]. In 1949, Ben Graham published a book on the principles of value investing, which Warren Buffet read at the age

[3] http://c250.columbia.edu/c250_celebrates/your_columbians/benjamin_graham.html

of 19. This book was called *The Intelligent Investor*. A few years later, Warren Buffett attended Columbia University Business School, primarily because he knew Ben Graham taught there. Warren eventually became a student of Ben Graham's, and the latter became the former's mentor.

And the rest is history.

It is safe to say that had Warren never met Benjamin Graham, we would not know who Buffett is today.

So (getting back to my story) of course I wanted to know everything about the man who taught "the man." So, I read every book on Ben Graham (and his investment principles) that I could get my hands on, deepening my knowledge of value investing that much more.

Okay. Let's fast forward a bit.

Whoosh….

I'm 19 years old, in college, and, over the course of 7 years (from age 12 to 19), I've basically spent all of my time reading every informational book on value investing ever written (well, not really, but you get my drift). I also read every book I could find on the investment philosophy's pioneers and most successful practitioners. So, now, I have all of this knowledge… but, once again, no *money*!

Which begs the question: *How the fuck am I going to put this new investment strategy to the test, if I have no* **moola** *to invest with*?

Crime was out of the question. At that point my parents had improved their lot in life through sheer hard work and determination, and had moved me and my siblings out of the ghetto, and into the picturesque suburbs of upstate New York. My parents had worked their asses off to give me and my younger siblings a shot at a better life. If I delved into any illegal activities (solely to make a quick buck) and ended up getting caught (*again*) it would crush them. And I'd never be able to live with myself.

No.

This time I had to make money the *right* way.

I looked around for some inspiration. And I quickly found it in my two mentors: My parents, and Warren Buffett. Both my parents and Warren had worked hard, and had saved their money, in order to improve their lifestyles.

Why couldn't I do the same?

I was smart. Industrious. Well-mannered (thanks to my parents). Surely someone would hire me, even if I did not have any work experience as of yet. And once I got a job, I would save my income until I had a nice, fat nest egg to invest with.

So, I sought employment.

And, as luck would have it, I found *two* jobs.

The first job was as a page, working at the local library in the town where I lived. The second job was as a student-worker at my college, a commuter school called Mercy College, located in Dobb Ferry, New York.

Because I went to college on scholarship, and because I still lived at home, rent-free, I basically had no expenses. So (as was my plan) I took a page out of Warren Buffett's book and saved every penny from my dual income. And by the time I had graduated college, four years later, I'd saved about $80,000.

And no one knew about it.

Here I was, 21-years-old, with eighty-Gs in the bank.

Fuck yeah!

Now, it was time to put this value investing strategy to the test.

One of the main tenants of the value investing approach is to never overpay for an *equity* (which is another fancy name for "stock" or "bond"). In fact, value investing teaches you how to find equities that are selling at a discount to their *intrinsic value* (which is another fancy name for "net worth"). The key thing is to buy stocks as you would groceries… WHEN THEY ARE ON SALE! This approach gives a value investor an advantage that no other investor-type has, called a *margin of safety* (which is another fancy way of saying "room for error").

So, short recap: Only buy stocks when they are selling at a discount to what they are really worth, because by doing so you inherently increase your margin of safety, and thus decrease your chances of failure.

Capisce?

Capisce!

Of course, there are other tenants in the value investing system that constitute a sort of algorithm. When all of these criteria are combined and put into effect, the results are astounding.

Anyway, I digress (sort of).

I went ahead and immediately opened an online brokerage account. Afterwards, I started to look for stocks to invest in. But, I suddenly ran into a roadblock. I couldn't find any companies to invest in. So, here I was, with a stack of cash, and an itchy trigger-finger, but I couldn't find a suitable target. Primarily because the majority of the businesses on the stock market simply did not meet my value investing standards. Most of the companies I was researching had poor business fundamentals, and/or were way too overpriced.

Fuck me.

Now, a non-value investor would've invested in lots of these companies, especially the Fortune 500 companies. Many investors think that it is wise to cram their stock portfolios with hundreds and thousands of companies. They do this because they think that by doing so they will build a diversified portfolio that will protect them against any major losses. That's probably true, but, all the same, a heavily diversified portfolio also hinders any considerable gains as well. I couldn't get Warren Buffett's voice out of my head: "Diversification is protection against ignorance. It makes little sense if you know what you're doing." [4] And Warren Buffett had backed these words with actions; there'd been plenty of times when he'd gone years without investing in a single stock because he could not find a company that met his investment standards. He refused to diversify his investment portfolio simply for the sake of diversification. He only invested in wonderful companies when they sold at attractive, value-generating prices.

So, I remained patient. Like my main man Warren.

The year was 2005. And the stock market had long rebounded from the panic-stricken, terrorist-skirmishing environment that had depressed it in September of 2001. Hopes were high. And so were stock prices. They called this a *bull* market (which is a term that denotes high optimism and stock purchasing activity in the equities marketplace). Just for the record, bull markets are NOT good for value investors. Why? Well, because during bull markets, prices tend to skyrocket, and therefore, nothing's on sale.

Let's fast forward again.

Whoosh…

2008. Good ole 2008. I know you remember what happened in December of 2008, people. *The Great Recession.* That's right. The 8 trillion-dollar housing bubble finally burst, sending all financial markets tumbling.

Including the stock market.

Yay!!

My patience had paid off. Because I had never stopped researching companies, I already had a list of suitable businesses that were ripe for investment. I hadn't been able to invest in them before, during the bull market of 2004-2007. But now that these companies' prices had plummeted, I could buy them, with the hopes of profiting handsomely when their prices rebounded.

[4] http://www.gurufocus.com/news/405554/a-young-warren-buffett-on-diversification

I was like a kid in a candy store.

I had saved an additional fifteen to twenty thousand dollars during the bull market (as I'd waited patiently for stock prices to drop), so I now had roughly $100,000 in my savings account. So, in March of 2009, during the throes of the market panic, I spent $50,000 acquiring shares of a media company with great fundamentals that had dropped to a deplorable 28 cents per share (from a high of $34.00 per share months earlier). All told, I bought roughly 178,570 shares of this media company. Then, I invested the remaining $50,000 that was in my savings account in a stalwart insurance company that had seen its stock price drop from $1,400 per share in May of 2007, to $7.00 per share in March of 2009, also due to the market panic.

Then... I waited.

And... the rest is history.

A year later, in 2010, as the market stabilized, somewhat, from the aftereffects of the crash, both stocks in my portfolio more than quadrupled in price. My media stock shot up to $4.35 per share, earning me profits of about $776,700. And my investment in the insurance company shot up to $57.00 per share, netting me a profit of precisely $357,094. All told, with two clicks of a mouse (the first click to buy the shares, the second click to sell the shares), I had turned my $100,000 nest egg into $1,133,877 in cold, hard cash.

My name is James Elie Pierre.

Today, as I write this book, I am 33 years old.

And I am retired (though still an entrepreneur—you never stop being an entrepreneur).

I do what *I* want with my time—not what a boss tells me to do.

I have a beautiful wife (and hope to have kids soon), and we spend our time vacationing around the world.

And I enjoy this lifestyle because I had the foresight to, first, work hard and save my earnings; second, exercise patience in waiting for the right investment opportunity to show up; and, third, implement the financial knowledge I'd learned to capitalize on certain investment opportunities when they finally *did* materialize.

The stock market is the fastest wealth-builder known to man... *when* it is utilized properly. I will show you how to use this investment vehicle to go from zero to a million in nine years or less. I started saving my first penny at 19 years old. And by age 27 (8 years later) I'd become a millionaire.

Take a walk with me.

I'll show you the pathway that leads to wealth and financial freedom.
But before I do, let me just say one more thing…

What This Book Is Not?

This book is **not** a get-rich-quick scheme.

So, if that's what you're after, you might as well go ahead and close this book and place it back on the shelf.

Becoming a millionaire is **not** easy.

Let me reiterate that again: **BECOMING A MILLIONAIRE IS *NOT* EASY!!**

It takes almost superhuman, mental discipline to make your first million. Trust me when I tell you that, while the personal finance guidelines in this book will be easy to understand, they will not be so easy to *apply*. In fact, they will be extremely difficult to implement. You will have to break poor money habits you've spent your entire life building. And you'll have to do it cold-turkey (if you want to reach a million in less than nine years). So, don't be fooled by the title of this book. The nine years I'm referring to are going to be the hardest—but most transformative—nine years of your life.

As the saying goes: "No pain, no profit!"

So, now that I've put that disclaimer out there, let's get started.

Let's turn you into a *millionaire*!!

CHAPTER 1

THE REAL MILLIONAIRES!

When you think of the word "millionaire," what is the first image that pops in your head?

Is it the image of a celebrity actor or actress? Perhaps, someone like Leonardo DiCaprio, or Jennifer Lawrence?

Or does the word conjure up images of your favorite athlete? Maybe LeBron James? Tom Brady? Tiger Woods? Cristiano Ronaldo?

Or do you think of other celebrity figureheads, such as Oprah Winfrey, Taylor Swift, Beyoncé Knowles, Justin Bieber, Kim Kardashian, Rihanna, or Jennifer Lopez?

If these are the people you think about when you hear the word "millionaire," I'm sure it's also hard not to think about the lavish lifestyle these celebrities lead. I mean, if you've got it, why not flaunt it, right?

For example, as I am writing these words, Oprah Winfrey just purchased a home in Telluride, Colorado[5]. But it's not just any home, people. This house cost the Big O $14 Million. The house sits on three acres of land (which, if we do the math, values each acre at $4.6 million). The house itself is 8,700 square feet. And this 5-bedroom, 6 ½ bath oasis also features the following:

[5] http://hookedonhouses.net/2015/12/22/15-unusual-features-in-oprah-winfreys-new-house/

- A heated driveway that never has to be plowed;
- Automated house systems that can be controlled from anywhere in the world;
- An interior, $150,000 fiber-optic, glass-plated hallway that changes colors;
- A 56-foot-long wine cellar that can hold approximately 1,600 bottles of wine;
- A $140,000 outdoor access bridge, with tree-top deck, that rises 35 feet above the ground;
- and, last but not least, a glassed-in observation tower that provides its owner with a panoramic, 360-degree view of the lush, Sophia Mountain Range (which, I heard, is breathtaking).

I think it's safe to say that if folks need to cross a privately-constructed access bridge in order to get to your house, you're officially ballin'.

Shit, I wonder if she charges visitors a toll?

But wait, there's more to being a millionaire than having a palatial mountain-side mansion with an access bridge. I mean, you can't be a *true* baller unless you have the whips to park outside that big house, right?

Take, for example, mega-athlete LeBron James.

I know he makes commercials for Kia. But check out what King James *really* has parked in his lot[6]. LeBron's Lamborghini Aventador, for example, has the following features:

- A price tag of $670,000;
- A 6.5 Liter, V-12 Engine;
- Heated mirrors;
- Telescopic steering wheel;
- and turbo shifts that let you go from 0-60 MPH in 2.9 seconds. (Check this out guys, I actually did the math on this one. If you blink once, slowly, when LeBron hits the gas pedal on his Lamborghini

[6] http://www.cheatsheet.com/automobiles/lebron-james-car-collection-10-vehicles-he-bought-and-forgot.html/?a=viewall

Aventador, the car will be ¾ of a mile down the road. And if you blink twice slowly, the car will nearly be out of sight. *What the fuck?!*)

And, because one car is not enough, King James also has a Ferrari F430 Spider, which he bought for around $217,000. This car has:

- An electric hood that renders the engine visible;
- A steering-wheel-mounted control system that allows its driver to control the car's electronic suspension, transmission options, and throttle responses;
- A roof panel that folds into the engine bay;
- Blah-di-blah, blah-di-blah, blah-di-blah…

You get the point.

But wait, guys. You can't be a *true* baller—even if you own palatial mansions that have privately-built access bridges, or own cars that move at the speed of light—if you don't *vacation* like a baller!

Take, for example, singing sensation and chart-topping heart-throb Justin Bieber.

As I am writing this, a few months ago, The Bieb went on a lavish vacation to Hawaii (and you can bet your ass he didn't fly coach, nor did he stay at the Motel 8, as I'll explain… right now).

Well, what were the highlights of this Hawaiian escapade? you may be asking yourself. Let's take a peek at Bieber's villa, which[7]:

- Cost $10,000 a night;
- Had an Olympic-sized, infinity swimming pool;
- Had a rooftop helipad (with—you can bet your ass—helicopter included);
- Had a private tennis court;
- Consisted of 3 stories, spanning 10,942 square feet;
- Had 5 bed rooms and 10 bathrooms;

[7] http://www.dailymail.co.uk/tvshowbiz/article-3722119/Go-big-home-Justin-Bieber-rents-huge-10k-night-mansion-Hawaii-rooftop-helipad-ferry-pals.html

- Stretched across 10 acres of land;
- Had 2 waterfalls and various ponds;
- Was equipped with a high-dive, 2-story waterslide;
- Blah-di-blah-di-blah-blah-blah…

You get the point, right? Big money-makers are big money-spenders. Living the high life. Soaking in sumptuous luxury. Painting the town red with money so green and long if you tied all their cash together you could tie a bow around the earth.

Is that what you think when you hear the word "millionaire"? Honestly?

Well, I have a secret to tell you. And you might not like it. But, the truth hurts.

Here is the secret: If you think the majority of millionaires are ballin', you are *wrong*.

In fact, the majority of millionaires live the opposite of the high life. That's right. They live the "low" life. (Though they are anything *but* low-lives). Meaning, the majority of millionaires live *below* their means. *Way* below their means.

Take our main guy, Warren Buffett, for instance…

HOW DID WARREN BUFFET SUCCEED?

At present, Warren is worth $76,000,000,000. That's right! Nine zeros. Not six. So, what did (or does) Warren Buffett do with all of his money? I'll tell you what he does with it.

He goes out of his way **not** to spend it. Here are a few examples:

- Warren still lives in the house he bought in 1958 for $31,000.
- Warren does not eat at fancy restaurants, but rather enjoys eating dollar burgers at McDonald's.
- Warren doesn't drink, or buy, liquor; his favorite beverage is Cherry Coke.

- Warren doesn't own fancy, luxury cars (in fact, he currently owns one 2014 Cadillac XTS, which he recently bought, after driving a beat-up 2006 Cadillac DTS for so many years).
- Warren Buffett has a flip phone, not a smart phone.
- Once, while staying in a hotel in New York for a business meeting, Warren called a friend and asked the friend to bring him a six pack of Coca-Cola, so that he wouldn't have to order room service (thus, saving himself a few bucks).
- In 2006, instead of spending millions of dollars on a fancy wedding (which he could have easily afforded to do), Warren instead got married at his daughter's house, in her living room.
- Warren doesn't have a personal driver; he instructs his friends to come pick him up at the airport whenever he's in town to visit them.

That's right. These are the daily habits of a man that has a personal net worth of $76 billion.

Pretty boring, huh?

Well, G-fucking golly. What's the point of having huge stacks of cash if you don't make it rain? you might be pondering.

Well, I'll let Warren Buffett explain what the point of being rich, and frugal, is. He had this to say about the topic at a past shareholder's meeting, and in a recent CNBC interview, respectively:

> There are things money can't buy. There's a point you start getting inverse correlation between wealth and quality of life. My life couldn't be happier. In fact, it'd be worse if I had six or eight houses. I have everything I need to have, and it doesn't make a difference after a point. [All I need is] good housing, good health, good food, good transport. When you get to 10 times, or 100 times, or 1,000 times, it doesn't make a difference [in quality of life].[8]

> Success is really doing what you love and doing it well. Really getting to do what you love to do every day—that's really the

[8] http://www.fool.com/investing/general/2014/06/08/warren-buffett-finally-explains-why-being-cheap-le.aspx

> ultimate luxury. Your standard of living is not equal to your cost of living.[9]

That's right. You heard correctly. Your *standard* of living is not equal to your *cost* of living.

Which, in layman's terms, means: You ain't gotta buy, or own, a whole bunch of material shit to be happy.

Many people think that in order to be truly happy, you have to own an exorbitant amount of material possessions. Nothing could be further from the truth. As Warren explains in the above quote, true happiness will come to you when you use your wealth to acquire the free time that you need to do what makes you happy. So, here's how the math looks:

- Material Possessions = Short Term Gratification + Eventual Poverty
- Wealth = Free Time + Long-term Happiness

The truly wealthy understand these equations and spend their time amassing wealth, not for the purpose of acquiring material desires, but rather, to achieve the financial independence that will allow them to spend their limited time on this earth doing what makes them *truly* happy. Like traveling. Or spending time with family and friends. Or donating to, and participating in, philanthropic endeavors. Etc.

Possessing a whole bunch of shit just to possess a whole bunch of shit will only lead to short-term happiness, and, very often, eventual poverty.

So, James, why did you mention all of those celebrity big-spenders at the beginning of this chapter? you might be wondering.

I opened the chapter speaking about luminary big-spenders because that is what the *media* wants you to believe being wealthy is all about. The media publishes and showcases such content, well, because it is entertaining. We *want* to hear about Justin Bieber's sprawling villa in Hawaii, and we want to see The Bieb chauffeuring his friends around in a private helicopter. We *want* to see LeBron James—driving off at the speed of light—in his brand-new Lamborghini Aventador.

I mean, how fucking cool is that?!

[9] http://www.investopedia.com/articles/financialcareers/10/buffett-frugal.asp

Not to mention, the product placement and marketing dollars these TV stations get whenever they mention a hot-ticket item. The end result? These media companies grab your attention, in order to raise their ratings, which then allows them to charge more for ad-dollars, thereby making them a fortune. Just from you watching their news report, or picking up their magazine, or whatever.

So, what's the trade-off?

Well, the media companies get richer by tickling your fancy for a few minutes. While you get a quick entertainment fix, but stay broke when it's all said and done.

Because, let's be honest, who wants to see news reports, or read in a magazine, about the *majority* of millionaires in this country, who are actually your small business owners, who work twelve hours a day and live in middle-class homes, and drive Camrys.

ZZZZZZZZZZZ…

Boring!

Exactly.

But in actuality, celebrity big-spenders only make up a fraction of the millionaires in this country. At present, there are 10,400,000 millionaires living in the United States[10]. Yet Forbes' "Highest-Paid Celebrity" millionaires list tops at 99[11]. So, it's safe to say that, in this country, the top 99 celebs represent only 0.000009% of the actual millionaire population.

So, basically, the media—in *their* representation of how millionaires live—is only, really showing you how less than 1% of millionaires live. Because if they chose to focus their media lens on the other 99.9% of millionaires in this country, well, let's face it: it wouldn't make for good entertainment. Which would then hurt their bottom line.

The title of this chapter is: *The Real Millionaires*. I gave it that title because, if we're going to succeed in turning you into a millionaire in nine years, the Warren Buffett way, then you have to know how *real* millionaires live.

Here are Warren Buffett's 2 famous rules for becoming (and staying) rich:

- Rule # 1: Never lose money!
- Rule # 2: Never forget Rule #1!

[10] http://www.cnbc.com/2016/03/07/record-number-of-millionaires-living-in-the-us.html
[11] http://www.forbes.com/celebrities/list/3/#tab:overall

That's what the majority of millionaires do. They work their asses off to make as much money as they can, then they spend the rest of their time spending as little of that money as they can. That's what it means to live below your means.

If your monthly expenses surpass your monthly income, you will *never* become a millionaire.

But, the more your monthly income surpasses your monthly expenses, the quicker you will become a millionaire.

So, it's fairly simple. Like most millionaires will tell you, it simply behooves you to do whatever it takes to make your income far outweigh your expenses. And now that you're just starting out, the easiest way to do that is to follow Rule #1: Never lose money. Or, rephrased: *Cut your fucking spending down to the bare minimum, goddamnit.*

I will teach you exactly how to efficiently cut all unnecessary spending out of your lifestyle in the next chapter, which is titled: *Chapter 2: The Budget.* But for now, let me expound a bit more on the traits and habits of real millionaires, in order to deepen your knowledge and understanding of who a true millionaire is.

Here are a list of 15 facts about millionaires that you may not know[12]:

- **Fact #1**: 80% of millionaires did not inherit their wealth; meaning, they went from $0 to $1 million the old-fashioned way, through hard work, frugal habits, and wise investments.
- **Fact #2**: 50% of millionaires are self-employed, or own a business; meaning, initially, they worked hard at a nine-to-five gig, then saved a majority of their income in order to invest in a small-business venture, or take advantage of a timely investment opportunity.
- **Fact #3**: The majority of millionaires drive used Fords, Cadillacs, and Lincolns; meaning, millionaires prefer not to spend money on luxury vehicles, because they understand that cars are poor investments, due to their depreciating characteristics.
- **Fact #4**: Only 20% of millionaires are retirees; meaning, 80% of millionaires still wake up every morning and go to work, either punching a clock for someone else, or managing their own small businesses.

[12] http://facts.randomhistory.com/millionaires-facts.html; http://www.moneypeach.com/20-millionaire-facts-you-did-not-know/

- Fact #5: A majority of millionaires are non-smokers; meaning, millionaires are attuned to the fact that if a 3-pack-per-day smoker invested their money, instead of spending it on cigarettes/tobacco/marijuana, in 46 years, that cigarette money, compounded through investments, would equal about $2,000,000 (so if you smoke, fucking quit! Now!).
- Fact #6: The majority of millionaires do not live in mansions, but, instead, live in homes valued, on average, at $300,000; meaning, real millionaires don't splurge on swanky pads, but instead buy comfortable, middle-class residences, which they then end up living in, on average, for over 20 years, thereby taking advantage of the increase in their home's equity.
- Fact #7: A century ago, there were only 5,000 millionaires in the USA, but now there are 10.4 million millionaires in our great country; meaning, people are achieving millionaire status at a faster rate than ever, due principally to an increase in access to information, technology, and financial markets (so, do yourself a favor—get educated, work hard, save, and invest in the right investments, because there's never been a better time than now to become a millionaire, and fairly quickly).
- Fact #8: The majority of millionaires' spouses/partners are just as, or more, frugal than they are; meaning, millionaires' spouses/partners hate to spend money unnecessarily (so, if you want to join the millionaire's club, make sure your significant other has the same financial goals as you do, and is willing to sacrifice short-term gratification, for long-term financial independence, because—and here's another fact for you—the number 1 reason for divorces in America stems from money issues).
- Fact #9: The majority of millionaires live on a monthly budget; meaning, millionaires know, beforehand, where each dollar will be allocated, and budget their income in a way that allows them to eliminate unnecessary spending, pay their necessary bills, save some money, and invest in business opportunities to achieve and expand their wealth (so, get ready to make some sacrifices, because budgeting is the most difficult terrain on the path to riches).

- Fact #10: The majority of millionaires don't use credit cards, and instead pay for almost everything with cash; meaning, millionaires are absolutely terrified of debt and stay away from it at all costs, unless it is positive debt, that is to say, the type of debt that can be used to finance positive cash-flow investments (like, for example, taking out a mortgage to buy a rental/investment property).
- Fact #11: While the average American watches over 5 hours of television per day, the average millionaire watches only 1 hour of television each day; meaning, the more time you spend sitting in front of that TV screen, the less time you have to do those things that will turn you into a millionaire, such as working, in order to increase your income and savings; or reading and learning about new financial strategies, in order to more quickly compound your savings and investments (come on, people, leave the idiot box alone and get with the program for Christ sakes).
- Fact #12: A majority of millionaires are bargain shoppers; meaning, whether they are buying groceries at Walmart, or purchasing businesses on the stock market, they look for discounts, and try never to spend money on unnecessary consumption or over-valued goods (so, get ready to cut some coupons).
- Fact #13: Studies show that millionaires are more preoccupied with sustaining their investment portfolios, than impressing strangers with their financial status; meaning, you'll never become a millionaire by trying to keep up with the Joneses (enough said).
- Fact #14: 80% of millionaires have completed college; meaning, they understand that a college degree will give them better access to a decent or high-paying job, which will allow them to maximize their savings in order to invest in business ventures or the stock market (so, don't be a fool—stay in school).
- Fact #15: 85% of millionaires started by investing no less than 20% of their work income; meaning, millionaires understand that saving isn't enough, and that money saved needs to be invested in order to quickly multiply (so quit spending your hard-earned dollars on shit you don't need, and develop the habit of paying yourself first and

placing those saved earnings in fruitful investment opportunities that will turn you into a millionaire in a jiffy).

So, still think being a millionaire is all about splurging on fancy homes, buying luxury cars, and vacationing around the world, first-class?

If you do, you're a moron!

Just kidding.

Actually, no, I'm not.

What I hope you now understand, after reading this chapter, is that real millionaires have one trait in common: frugality. That is to say, they do not spend their hard-earned money on unnecessary purchases—especially when they are first starting out building their wealth. The media, of course, would have you believe differently, for their own selfish gains. But don't let the idiot box fool you. If you want to become a millionaire, you have to work as hard as possible, save as much money as possible, and invest as often as possible, especially in the beginning.

So, James, you ask, *does that mean I can't enjoy the fruits of my labor* ***until*** *I actually reach millionaire status*?

No. Not at all. By all means, enjoy the fruits of your labor. All work and no play is not healthy, either. What I'm saying is, be mindful of *how* you play. So, for example, if you want to go on a vacation from time to time, that's fine and dandy. But go on an *affordable* vacation that is not going to set you back financially, or put you in debt.

Understand that your spending habits are what will make you, or break you. The more you spend your money on shit you don't really need, the longer it will take you to become a millionaire. Whereas, the less you spend (and the more you save and invest), the quicker you'll become a millionaire.

Becoming rich is a formula. It's an exact science. Not a theory. And it is obtainable. If it weren't, the population of millionaires wouldn't have ballooned the way it has in the past hundred years.

So, to recap, if you want to become a millionaire quickly, first, stop spending; second, start working and saving; and third, invest those savings in profitable investment opportunities on a regular basis.

But I love to buy stuff, James. Really, I do. It makes me happy; it makes me feel all warm and fuzzy inside, you might be thinking.

Yeah, yeah. I know. It's true. Buying the latest car, the latest smart-phone, or a brand-new home entertainment system does *feel* good, doesn't it?

But for how long does it feel good? I'll tell you how long. Until the next, hot-ticket item comes out on the market. And then you forget about that first feel-good purchase, and now suddenly you can't wait to get your hands on that newer item the idiot box is telling you everyone has.

You're right, James, you might be thinking. *But, how do I curb my desire for unnecessary purchases, like real millionaires do, in order to maximize my savings and investments, so I can join the millionaire's club, too?*

Well, there's an answer for that too. It's called budgeting. And we'll cover that in the next chapter.

Shall we....

CHAPTER 2

THE BUDGET!

You now can identify a *real* millionaire (as opposed to the "Hollywood" millionaire, whose prodigal exploits are romanticized by the media for advertisement dollars). And by now, you also have an idea of how a *real* millionaire views money (not as a means to buy lavish toys that eventually lead to the squandering of his/her wealth, but rather as a tool to secure and maintain financial independence).

Now it's time to discuss the foundation upon which all wealth is built and sustained.

The Budget.

Let me put it this way: If wealth were a tree, the budget would be the roots. And if wealth were the atmosphere, the budget would be gravity. The budget is what keeps prospective millionaires, and millionaires alike, grounded. I could write you a check for a gazillion dollars, today, and without a budget, you'd lose it all inside of a week (like most lottery winners do). The lack of a practical budget is why broke people never become rich, and why rich people oftentimes go broke.

The budget is your anchor; it keeps you from floating away into unfriendly waters.

The budget is your foundation; it keeps you balanced, stable and sure-footed.

The budget should be the first tool that you master in your quest to become rich; or else your road to riches will quickly become an unpaved jungle, with vile and gruesome predators lurking behind every shrub, pouncing on you and knocking you off course every chance they get.

Have I made myself fucking clear?!

Good!

Seriously, people. Out of all of the tools wealthy persons use to get and stay rich, the budget is the most significant.

Merriam-Webster's dictionary defines the word "budget" as: "A plan used to decide the amount of money that can be spent, and how it will be spent."[13] Which brings to mind a famous quote by the great Benjamin Franklin, who said: "If you fail to plan, you are planning to fail."

Now, Benjamin Franklin did not end up on our $100 bill for no reason. He was a smart fellow, that Ben Franklin. I mean, he *was*, among other things, one of the founding fathers of this great country, for crying out loud. Franklin was also a scientist, an inventor, a politician/political theorist, a published author, a civic activist, a statesman, and a U.S. ambassador.

Again, I digress. I'm sorry. (Though, by now, you're probably used to it).

My point is, Benjamin Franklin wasn't a quack. The man knew what he was talking about. And his advice on planning couldn't be more important or quintessential to an individual whose goal it is to become a millionaire.

So, moving right along.

The budget, in essence, is a plan. It is a plan that will help you determine *how much* of your income you should spend, and *where* you should spend that money.

There are hundreds of books written by hundreds of authors on the topic of budgeting. Many of these volumes are as thick as textbooks; massive, gargantuan tomes on how to successfully structure your personal finances.

Fuck all that shit.

If you want to stop misspending or over-spending (and you *need* to stop misspending and over-spending if you're gonna give yourself a shot at becoming a millionaire), I am going to tell you five places where you should spend your hard-earned money. These five spending places will represent your entire budget. So, know that every time you spend money outside of these five

[13] http://www.merriam-webster.com/dictionary/budget

places, you are simply delaying that splendid day when you finally become a millionaire. The five destinations for your income should be:

1. **S**avings
2. **T**ransportation
3. **N**ecessary Bills
4. **G**roceries
5. **I**nvestments

I call it the STNGI Budget (pronounced *Stingy*). Every time you get paid, a percentage of your income should, first, go into a savings account; second, pay for the transportation costs associated with traveling to work; third, pay off necessary bills; fourth, pay for necessary grocery items; and lastly (when you've saved enough money), buy investments.

HOW DID WARREN BUFFET SUCCEED?

Before I expound on each item on the budget list, I'd like to cite a few passages from Roger Lowenstein's biography on Warren Buffett, *Buffett: The Making of An American Capitalist*, the book that changed my life. I want to highlight these passages because, in the past, whenever I was tempted to stray from my budget, I would think about the following stories about Warren Buffett, and it would strengthen my resolve:

> Another time, when [Warren Buffett and Katherine Graham] landed at La Guardia [airport], Graham was in a hurry to make a telephone call and asked [Warren] if he had a dime. Buffett fished a quarter out of his pocket. Not wanting to waste the fifteen cents, he started [going outside] to change [the quarter] … Graham hollered "*Warren*, give me that quarter."

> The Buffetts [Warren, his wife Susie, and their newborn daughter] started out in a $65-a-month... apartment. Given Warren's promises of riches, Susie may have been a bit taken aback. The place was so run-down that mice crawled into their shoes at night. Warren was so tight about money that when the couple had their first daughter... they made a bed for her in a dresser drawer.

Now, here is Warren who (for example, in the second excerpt cited above) was not quite yet a millionaire, but he wasn't broke either. The year was 1952, and Warren probably had close to half a million dollars (in today's money) saved up. But his goal to become a millionaire forced him to impose a strict budget on his lifestyle, which resulted in his denying himself, as well as his loved ones, the merest banalities.

Now, don't get it twisted. I'm not telling you to make change for quarters, or forgo the purchasing of a crib, in favor of placing your baby in a dresser drawer, simply to save a few bucks. That's not the message I want to get across with these stories about Warren Buffett. What I *do* want you to understand is that, if you really want to become a millionaire quickly, be prepared to make extreme sacrifices.

Be prepared to pinch those pennies harder than you've ever pinched them before.

Many of your friends, family and associates will not understand the financial sacrifices you'll be making, especially in the beginning. But have faith in your resolve. Believe in your goal. Keep your eyes fixed on the finish line (which is that day, nine years from today, or less, when you can finally retire with $1 million in the bank). Yes, it is easier said than done. But understand that, with the help of a fine-tuned budget, no financial goal is impossible.

So, let's explore, in more detail, the components of STNGI, your new budget.

1. SAVINGS ACCOUNT

A savings account is essential if you plan to become a millionaire. Why? Well, because the money you deposit into your savings account is the seed capital that will create your fortune.

If you have a job, but are still living paycheck to paycheck, I'll tell you why that is: **YOU DON'T PAY YOURSELF FIRST**!

Pay myself first? What in god's name are you talking about, James? you may be asking yourself.

Well this is what the fuck I'm talking about: Your boss hands you a check, and you turn around and hand that entire check to Macy's, Neiman Marcus, Coach, Michael Kors, Applebee's, TGI Fridays, Best Buy, Walmart, Target, Home Depot, Visa, American Express, and a slew of other corporate entities preying on your consumerist desires. And then you look up and a month has gone by, and you're just as broke as you were the month before. And then you start to bitch and complain about not getting paid enough at your job. But you fail to realize what wealthy people the world over have always understood, and that is: It's not how much you make, but rather, how much you *keep*, that will determine your financial success. You could have a $1 million per year salary, but what good is that going to do you if you're spending $1.5 million per year at retail stores. At that rate, you'll simply find yourself racking up half-a-million dollars in credit card debt every year. So, it's not the largeness of your salary that's the problem, but rather, your non-compliance with the first law of personal finance: Save a portion of your income.

So, if you don't have a savings account, I advise you to open one up.

Now!

And every time your boss hands you a check, before paying anyone else with your hard-earned money, *pay yourself first*. Take 10%-20% of your paycheck and deposit it into your savings account. Immediately. The most efficient way to accomplish this is to go to a bank that is somewhat out of your way, and ask to speak to the personal banker there. (You do not want to have easy access to your savings account as you are building it up. That is why it is prudent to open your savings account at a bank or credit union that is inconveniently far away). Tell the personal banker at this far-away bank that you would like to open a savings account. He or she will help you do so promptly.

Then, once you're done opening your savings account, visit your job's Human Resources department. Give your HR administrator the number to your savings account, and ask him/her to automatically deposit anywhere between 10%-20% of your pay into that savings account. Trust me. You won't even miss the money. I call this forced savings. And for those of you who do not yet have the mental discipline or resolve to manually save a portion of your income on a regular basis, this is the best route you can take.

You should always try to deposit at least 10% of your income into your savings account. Of course, the more you deposit into your savings account, the quicker you will achieve that coveted millionaire status, but, nonetheless, anywhere between 10% and 20% is a good starting point. When I first started saving, I was so psyched out by the idea of becoming a millionaire that I deposited over 65% of my paycheck into my savings account, denying myself all consumerist pleasures for about 3 (very long) years. But the way I looked at it was, if I had to sacrifice buying a new flat-screen TV for the moment, in exchange for absolute financial freedom in the near future, I'd gladly do so. Over and over again. Without a single regret. And without a single care about how others viewed me.

So, to recap, the first recipient of your income should be your savings account. If you don't already have one, go open one up at the bank as soon as possible. Then, once you've opened your savings account, make it a priority to *pay yourself first* (before spending money on anything else, including important bills). Accomplish this by automatically depositing between 10% to 20% of each paycheck—and/or any other forms of income—into that savings account. Period. No ifs, ands, or buts.

But, reader, beware.

Once you start saving money, in time, two things are going to happen. First, you are going to be impressed by the amount of increasing cash in your savings account. And second, you are going to be tempted to spend a little bit of that large quantity. Well...

DO NOT TOUCH THE MONEY!

Think of it this way. If wealth were a tree, the few dollars you deposit into your savings account are the seeds from which that tree will grow. And every time you take a dollar out of your savings account (for any reason other than to invest it), you are merely plucking a seed out of the ground, and thereby delaying, or outright preventing, your tree from blossoming. So, I reiterate: **Do not** touch the money in your savings account (unless it is for the purpose of investing it)!

Okay. Good.

Now that we've gone over the first component of your new budgetary plan (which is the savings account), let's move onto the next component: Transportation.

2. TRANSPORTATION

The second place you should spend your income is transportation.

Now, hold on. Hear me out, buddy. Because *your* definition of the word "transportation" and my definition of the word might be slightly different.

The type of transportation *I'm* talking about is *not* the kind where you jet-set around the world, spending your hard-earned money on lavish vacations. No. I'm also not talking about the kind of transportation costs that include splurging on taxi and bus fares to go make it rain in downtown nightclubs, two or three times a week.

No. No. No.

If you want to become a millionaire really, really fast, the only time you should be hopping in your car, or paying public transportation fares, is to go to work, the grocery store, or to the doctors.

Remember what I said before, earlier in this chapter, about what it takes to become a millionaire? Heart-wrenching sacrifice. And the type of sacrifice I'm referring to will need to be manifested in the form of uncompromising, superhuman self-control.

Listen, guys and gals. Neither fuel, nor public transportation fares, are cheap nowadays. On average, it costs $43.25 to fill a mid-size sedan's tank[14]. And for mid-size SUVs and pick-up trucks, the average cost to fill up a tank can range from $69 to over $100, depending on oil prices[15]. Also, non-private transportation isn't cheap either. The national average for taxi fares, particularly in busy, metropolitan areas, is around $10.50 per mile. Ten *fucking* dollars per mile! (Shit, that being the case, I'd rather *crawl* to my destination, no matter how fucking long it took me to get there).

So, you see. It ain't cheap to move around (at least, not like it used to be). So, it behooves a prospective millionaire (that would be you) to cut down on his/her daily excursions. Because the less you drive, the more of your income you get to keep, and the more dough you keep, the more you can save, and the more you save, the more you can invest, and the more you invest, the quicker you'll become a millionaire.

Got it?

Good.

[14] http://www.aol.com/finance/?gen=1

[15] http://www.cars.com/go/advice/Story.jsp?section=fuel&story=fuelCost&subject=fuelList

So, let's recap. While transportation costs are a necessary expense in life, if you want to become a millionaire sooner rather than later, you should limit your excursions to the bare minimum, strictly speaking: (1) going to work (in order to earn money to pay for your living expenses); (2) going to the grocery store (to buy necessary food and clothes to live); and (3) the occasional doctor's visit (to maintain a healthy lifestyle). Any other outing is considered a social outing, and therefore deemed unnecessary. So, heed this quote from Blaise Pascal, the French mathematician, physicist, philosopher, and inventor: "*All of humanity's problems stem from man's inability to sit quietly in a room alone.*" In other words, if you want to avoid temptation, trouble, trials, and tribulations (all of which are impediments to a prospective millionaire's goals) then sit… your… ass… at… home. And save the social outings for that day when you finally have a cool million dollars chillin' in your bank account.

Capisce?

Capisce!

Let's move right along, then, to the third component of the STNGI budget: Necessary Bills.

3. NECESSARY BILLS

Like transportation costs, there are two types of bills: necessary bills and unnecessary bills. If you want to become a millionaire quickly, then you have to cut your monthly bills down to the bare minimum. That means using your income to pay off *necessary* monthly expenses, as opposed to accumulating expenses that the idiot box tricks you into *thinking* are necessary.

So, for example. In this day and age, we all need cellphones. That's simply a fact of life. But do you *really* need the newest model iPhone, which will end up costing you $175 (or more) per month? Or can you get by with an earlier model smart phone with a prepaid plan that will cost you only $45 per month? Most of us need cars, in order to commute to work and so forth. But do you *really* need a brand-new Audi A8, whose car note will end up costing you over $500 per month? Or can you get by with a used Ford, which will only set you back about $100 per month? As much as I hate it, the idiot box does have some value. Television helps us keep up with the news, and, from time to time, it does provide us with educational programming. But do you *really* need to have a comprehensive cable package containing every channel known to man for $200 plus per month? Or can you get by on a basic internet/cable package that'll end up costing you no more than $75 per month?

Get my drift?

Yes, we all have to pay bills. But, if you really want to, you can always find strategic ways to cut down, or (even better) eliminate certain bills altogether. That is how *real* millionaires think.

Increase income.

Decrease monthly liabilities.

Accumulate assets.

To help you differentiate between necessary and unnecessary bills, I've compiled a list of what your monthly expenses should look like. If you stay within the boundaries of this list, it will help you execute your STNGI budget with the utmost efficiency. On the other hand, if you stray from this bare-bones list, you'll find yourself accruing expenses you don't really need, thereby delaying your early-retirement day!

This is what your monthly expenses should look like:

1. <u>**Savings**</u>: Pay yourself first. (Accomplish this by putting 10-20% of your income in a savings account).
2. <u>**Shelter**</u>: Pay your rent and/or mortgage. (If you rent, try to keep your rent under $1,000/month; and if you own a home, try to keep your mortgage payments under $1,750/month).
3. <u>**Utilities**</u>: Pay your electricity and water bills. (But try to keep these costs down—to about $100/month—by minimizing the use of your electricity and water).
4. <u>**Cable/Internet**</u>: Pay your cable and internet bill. (But try to keep this bill under $80/month by getting a simple, basic package deal—don't forget, *real* millionaires don't watch much television anyway).
5. <u>**Car Note**</u>: Pay your car note. (Keep this bill under $150 by owning/leasing an earlier model, non-luxury vehicle).
6. <u>**Car Insurance**</u>: Pay your car insurance. (Try to keep this bill under $100/month by owning a cheap car and getting cheap, online insurance; there are some companies that offer insurance for as low as $30/month, however just make sure you drive carefully).
7. <u>**Cellphone**</u>: Pay your cellphone bill. (Keep this bill under $75, by buying an earlier model smartphone with a cheap, pre-paid plan).

8. **Debt**: Pay off your debt on time, and refrain from accumulating any more debt. (Try to devote at least 20% of your income to paying off any consumer debt or school loans you might have).

So, there you have it. The 8 fixed expenses listed above should constitute the entirety of your *necessary* monthly bills. If you're paying any other recurring bills, outside of the 8 bills mentioned above, then you're simply throwing away money. The 8 expenses mentioned above are essential to your livelihood. You need to save money; you need a roof over your head with functioning utilities; you need the TV/internet, to a certain extent, in order to keep up with what's going on in the world; you need a car, with viable insurance, to facilitate transportation to work and so forth; you need a phone in order to communicate with others; and you need to pay off your debt obligations, in order to keep your credit intact.

And that's *all* you need!

Sorry to say, but you don't *need* a gym membership to live. And you definitely don't *need* a Macy's store membership to survive. Don't confuse what you *need* with what you *want*. The less you concentrate on what you want, and the more you focus on paying for only what you need, the quicker your financial fortune will turn around. Your bank account will grow exponentially. And life will become simpler.

So, to recap. The only monthly, fixed expenses you should have are (1) savings, (2) shelter, (3) utilities, (4) cable/internet, (5) car payment, (6) car insurance, (7) phone, and (8) debt obligations. And only 1 out of those 8 monthly expenses should you try to maximize: savings. For the other 7 categories, you should try to minimize them as much as possible, and deposit whatever money you save by doing so into your… (you guessed it!)… *savings account*.

Let's keep it moving.

The next item on our budget is Groceries. Let's explore this in a bit more detail.

4. GROCERIES

Okay, guys. What I am about to say is going to piss some people off. Primarily because it will be asking a lot of you. I'm going to ask you to give up something that you've been doing, habitually, your entire life. And if you *do* give it up, you'll become a millionaire, virtually, overnight (okay, I'm exaggerating a little, but you get my drift). And while not giving it up will not eliminate your chances of becoming a millionaire, altogether, it *will* delay your retirement day more than any other one-time expense known to man.

So, here is one of the most essential secrets to becoming a millionaire fast: Don't eat out.

When you eat out at restaurants, you are merely throwing money away. Damn near literally.

Explain how that works, James, you might be thinking right now.

Okay. I will.

A large pizza at Pizza Hut will run you $14.99. But you can get an any-topping, large pizza at your local Walmart Super Center for as low as $4.00. Savings: $10.00.

Cha-Ching!

A spaghetti with meat sauce entrée at Olive Garden will cost you $10.59 (not including tip). But if you were to buy the ingredients for that same meal at your local Walmart Super Center , it would cost you a total of $5.25 ($2.00 for a box of spaghetti + $3.15 for meat sauce). Savings: $5.34.

Cha-Ching!

A Jack Daniels Salmon & Grilled Shrimp Scampi meal at TGI Fridays will cost you $17.59 (not including liquor and tip). But if you were to buy the ingredients for that same meal at your local grocery store, it would cost you a total of $10.56 ($8 for a pound of salmon + $2.56 for a package of shrimp scampi). Savings: $7.03.

And for you liquor-lovers out there, a single shot of Patron Tequila at your local bar will cost you, on average, $12.00. *Per shot!* Whereas, if you were to walk/drive your lazy ass to the neighborhood package store, you could buy an *entire bottle* of Patron Tequila for $50.00. So, to simplify this for you: That same $50.00 would get you approximately 4 shots at a restaurant/bar establishment. *4* shots! I'm no math whiz, here. But I think getting an entire bottle for $50.00 beats getting 4 shots for $50.00. So, if an entire bottle holds approximately 16 shots, at a bar, those 16 shots would cost you roughly $192.00. As opposed to getting a bottle for $50.00 at the liquor store. Savings: $142.00.

Cha-Ching!
Cha-Ching!
Cha-Ching!

Cha-Ching!

Here's the deal, guys and gals. It may not seem like it, but you're spending a *fortune* on eating and drinking out. That's why it is very important, from here on out, to eliminate restaurant and bar outings from your daily itinerary.

When it comes to food, the only place you should be purchasing your foodstuff is at the grocery store. And even then, you should be bargain shopping. Instead of buying the brand-name food products, buy the store brands—they're much cheaper. And start cutting coupons, people. You'll be surprised how much you can save by utilizing coupons.

So, to recap. Stop throwing money away by eating and drinking out. Make a firm decision, right now, to only eat out once per month. The rest of your time should be spent bargain shopping at your local grocery store; buy store brands and use coupons to maximize your savings. And if you have to drink (which, really, you don't), buy your liquor at the local liquor store, instead of paying 10, 15, 20 times more for the same goddamn drink at a bar/restaurant.

It ain't rocket science, people. The only person getting rich when you eat out is the restaurant owner. Not you. So buy some groceries and stay your ass at home. And in the future, when you become a millionaire, maybe you can own your own restaurant and up-charge the shit out of ignorant suckers. But in the meantime, don't be a sucker yourself.

Got it?

Good.

Moving right along. Let's discuss the 5th and final component of your new budget: Investments.

5. INVESTMENTS

You can save your money. And you can budget your expenses. But unless you *invest* those savings, you'll never become a millionaire. At least, not quickly.

When you invest your cash, what you are doing, essentially, is buying an asset that will multiply your money over time. The most common asset classes are businesses, real estate, and (the topic of this book) equities—meaning stocks, bonds, etc. I've seen individual stock traders (some of whom are my good friends) make in upwards of $100,000 *per day* in profits. Of course, many of them are *day* traders. Day trading is a very risky, but profitable, type of stock market investing. This book is not about day trading. What I will teach you about in this book is a form of stock market investing called *value* investing. Though the latter strategy may take a bit more time to yield results, it carries way less risk, and therefore is a more dependable strategy.

I am not going to spend too much time talking about investments in this section, because we are going to discuss it at length later on this book. But understand that if you do not invest (wisely), it will be virtually impossible for you to become a millionaire in nine years or less. That is why investments are a critical part of your budget.

So, to recap. Once you've saved a good amount of money, and have preserved those savings by strictly budgeting the remainder of your income (by spending your earnings only on *necessary* transportation, bills, and groceries), keep in mind that you will have to invest your saved income in order to reach $1,000,000. And the best way to invest that income—when it comes to investing in the stock market—is by using the value investing strategy.

Copacetic?

Great!

Chapter Recap

So, ladies and gents. If you want to become a millionaire, you're going to have to budget your money. There's no way around it. And understand that the more strictly you budget your expenses, the more quickly you will become a millionaire.

When you get paid, your money should go to 5 places, and 5 places alone. I call it the STNGI (pronounced *stingy*) budget. The 5 places your money should go are:

1. Savings account: Pay yourself first by depositing between 10-20% of your paycheck, immediately, in this account.
2. Transportation: Purchase gas, or public-transportation fares, to commute strictly to work, the grocery store, and to the occasional doctor's visit; otherwise, sit your ass at home!
3. Necessary Bills: Your monthly bills should cover the following 8 expenses (and nothing more): (1) Savings (2) Shelter (3) Utilities (4) Internet/Cable (5) Car Note (6) Car Insurance (7) Phone (8) Debt Obligations. (Also, try to maximize your savings contributions, while minimizing—to the best of your ability—the other 7 monthly expenses).
4. Groceries: Do not eat out at restaurants anymore; maximize your savings by grocery shopping and eating strictly at home. (Also, make sure to buy store brands, instead of brand-name grocery products, and use as many coupons as possible).
5. Investments: Once you've saved a large amount of money, plan to invest it wisely in the stock market (which I will show you how to do later on in this book), by utilizing value investing strategies.

CHAPTER 3

THE GAME PLAN!

If you want to become a millionaire, you have to have an income that can support your savings goals, while also allowing you to pay for your living expenses.

Let me cut to the chase and tell you the three-step process we are going to use to turn you into a millionaire in nine years:

- STEP 1: Secure an income that allows you to save at least $300 a week;
- STEP 2: After securing this income, save $300 per week for the next three years, for a total of $46,800;
- STEP 3: After three years of saving, spend the next six years growing your $46,800 at a rate of 70% per year, using the value investing system, to achieve a total return of $1,129,638 at the end of six years.

That is the game plan, people. It's as simple as that. As you can see, in nine years (maybe less), I'll take you from $0 to just a little over $1 million.

Deal?

Cool.

How Did Warren Buffet Succeed?

Before we delve further into the components of the game plan, let's explore Warren Buffett's views on it. Did he have a similar approach to our game plan, which consists of securing an ample income that will allow you to save plentifully, in order to invest your way to $1 million? Again, here are some excerpts from Roger Lowenstein's biography, *Buffett: The Making of An American Capitalist*, the book that changed my life:

> Warren would sit on the fire escape at Rosehill elementary school and flatly tell his chums that he would be rich before he was thirty-five.... Warren was charting his way towards a financial goal.
>
> When Warren was six... Warren managed to buy six-packs of Coke for twenty-five cents; then he waddled around... selling the sodas at five cents each, for a nickel profit.
>
> [At age 13] Warren's... life revolved around his job as a carrier for the *Washington Post*. He kept a record of his earnings... from his paper route... [and] far from relinquishing the paper route, he expanded it. He promptly procured a route with the *Times-Herald*, the *Post's* morning competitor, covering the same territory as he had with the *Post*.... Soon Warren had five delivery routes and close to five hundred papers to deliver each morning.... Leila [his mother] would arise early to make him breakfast; Warren was out the door by [5:20 AM] to catch the bus... On the rare occasion when he was ill, Leila did the route, but she didn't go near the money. "Collections were everything to him," [Leila stated]. "You didn't dare touch the drawer where he kept his money. Every penny had to be there."

> Warren had turned his paper routes into a business. He was earning [$2,200 in today's money, every] month—what many a young man was earning as a full-time wage—and [he was] saving every dime. In 1945, when he was still only fourteen, he took [today's equivalent of $15,500] of his profits and invested it in forty acres of Nebraska farmland.
>
> In their senior year [of high school, Warren and his friend Danly] bought a used pinball machine for [$250 in today's money] .... Warren had an idea: why not put the machine in the barbershop on Wisconsin Avenue and rent it out? Warren approached the barber, who agreed to a fifty-fifty split. At the end of the first day, they found [$150 in today's money] in the machine. Within a month or so, Warren and Danly had machines in three barbershops. Prospering, they expanded to seven... "Eventually we were making [$530 in today's money] a week," [Warren] recalled.
>
> Warren graduated [high school] in June 1947... He had delivered almost 600,000 newspapers and in the process earned over [$52,000 in today's money]. Money was coming in from newspapers, from Wilson Coin Op [Warren and Danly's pinball machine business], and from a Nebraska tenant farmer.
>
> By [the end of college] ... From all his ventures combined, Warren had saved [$95,000 in today's money]. That trifling grubstake would be the source of every dollar that Buffett would earn.
>
> ... since leaving college in 1950... Buffett, quietly investing on his own [in the stock market], had boosted his personal capital from [$95,000, in today's money] to [$1.3 million, in today's money, by the year 1956].

As you can see, the common thread that permeated Warren Buffett's early life was, firstly, his desire to work extremely hard (sometimes holding multiple jobs and possessing a few start-up businesses, all at the same time) in order to maximize his income levels. Secondly, Warren had an unwavering resolve to save (without compromise) as close to 100% of his earnings as possible. And lastly, Warren was willing to invest those savings in the stock market in order to multiply his cash (using the value investing approach) on his way to becoming a millionaire.

So, did Warren Buffet follow our game plan in order to achieve success? You're fucking right he did!

Now, let's discuss the three components of our game plan—work income, savings, and investments—in more detail.

STEP 1: WORK INCOME

Almost every great businessperson that I know of, personally, or whom I've read about in books, did not inherit his/her wealth. Instead, these millionaires held regular 9 to 5 jobs in the beginning. And from those jobs, they saved a large portion of their earnings, in order to invest in the business of their choice later on.

Many people view their jobs as some kind of misfortune. We hate having to get up early to go punch a clock, in order to work long, laborious hours, for what we believe to be meager pay.

I know.

It sucks.

But let me tell you something. It's about time that you stopped looking at your job as some form of bad luck, and started seeing your employment for what it truly is: your liberator. Your job is your liberator because it provides you with seed money. The dictionary defines "seed capital" as: "money that is used for starting a new business, program, project, etc."[16] Our project of interest is turning you into a millionaire. And I know you've heard the saying: "It takes money to make money." Well, where do you think most millionaires find the initial cash that they need to either start their own businesses, or take advantage of a timely investment opportunity?

Uh… *duh*!

[16] https://www.merriam-webster.com/dictionary/seed%20capital?utm_campaign=sd&utm_medium=serp&utm_source=jsonld

Their *9 to 5* income. *That's* where.

It's really not that hard of a concept to understand. I mean, unless you know a financial benefactor who is willing to give away their hard-earned money; or, unless you know of a bank that is willing to open up their vaults and rain cash down on you to get your investment plans afoot; or, unless you're Harry Potter and you have a magic fucking wand that can make money appear (*poof!*) like a rabbit out of a hat…

… unless you have access to one or all of these arcane advantages, you're going to have to build your fortune like everybody else did: through hard work. And I say *hard* work, because, if you're going to become a millionaire in nine years or less, you are going to need a work income that is ample enough to pay your bills, *and* allow you to save roughly $300 per week.

There you have it, folks.

I never said this was going to be easy. (In fact, I remember telling you the opposite, that the quest to $1,000,000 was going to be the hardest, but most gratifying, experience of your life).

Well, you must be thinking, *James, how the fuck am I going to find a job that provides me with enough income to cover my bills* **and** *save 300 bucks a week?*

Maybe the answer doesn't lie in a job. At least not a *single* job. What I'm saying is, you picked up this book because you wanted to know how Warren Buffett did it, right? (Hell, that's the fucking title of the book, ain't it—*How Did Warren Buffett Succeed?*) Well, I'm *telling* you how he did it. And scores of millionaires around the world followed the same blueprint. They all started with multiple jobs. One full-time job to help pay the bills. And another part-time job, or side business, to save money.

For those readers who are still very young, don't forget Fact #14 about real millionaires, which I mentioned in Chapter 2. About 80% of real millionaires are college graduates. Reason being, you can get a higher paying job with a college degree. So for those of you who are young enough and still can, complete high school and go to college, and get your degree in a field that pays a boatload of money. If you do that, you may not need to have more than one job; you'll be able to save for your retirement, *and* pay your living expenses, from one salary.

But for the rest of you who are probably halfway through life, going back to school to get a higher paying degree may not be an option anymore. And if that's the case, if you want to increase your income in order to maximize your savings, you're going to have to get up off your lazy ass, and go apply for a second job. And, by the way, it doesn't matter what that second part-time or full-time job is. Go flip burgers at McDonald's or Wendy's. Go make sandwiches at a Subway Restaurant. Go fold sweaters at a retail clothing store. Go greet customers at Walmart. Go sell cars at a car dealership. Go man the cash register at ShopRite.

I don't care what the hell you do.

As long as that second job can net you at least $300 per week, that's all that matters.

If Warren Buffett himself needed more than one job to maximize his earnings and savings, chances are you're going to need more than one income as well. And make no mistake about it: Whether or not you accomplish this part of the game plan will say a lot about your character. I'm sorry, but I have to speak the truth. You did not buy this book to get lied to. If—despite whatever personal shit you may be going through in your life right now—you're able to maximize your income by holding two or more jobs (or, by sacrificing your free time to work lots of overtime hours at your current job, in order to increase your pay), that says that you are truly committed to becoming a millionaire, and have the strength of character required to accomplish this lofty goal.

But if, on the other hand, for whatever reason, you can't muster up enough mental and physical fortitude to maximize your work income, though it pains me to say it, you might as well give up now. Raise the white flag, and go and join the millions of dreamers who'd rather sit on their fat asses and scratch lotto tickets, in the *hope* of striking it big.

It takes money to make money. Period. So, you can either get up and go make more money; or, you can continue *wishing* you had more money.

The choice is yours.

So if you belong to the former group of go-getters, get the fuck up right now and go increase your work income. Work longer hours at your current job if you have to. Go get a part-time gig if need be. Go get another full-time job if you can. Start a side business if you have the resources to do so. But whatever you do, increase your income so that you are able to save at least $300 per week. Because in nine years or less, that $300 you're putting away every week is going to liberate you. It's going to provide you with the financial independence that you always craved. In nine years or less, you will no longer have to deal with a cruel boss and hectic work environment. You'll no longer have to slave to make someone *else* rich.

That's right!

You'll never have to suffer these plights again!

Because when you finally become a millionaire, you'll be your own boss, and what you do with your own time will be up to you. You can spend as much time as you want with your beautiful wife/husband, and children. You can take care of your parents the way they deserve to be taken care of. You can travel the world and become enlightened by all of the splendid wonders it has to offer. You can donate as much money and time as you'd like to philanthropic causes, in order to help those in need.

Or, you can do what I do sometimes (ok, maybe more than just sometimes): You can wake up, shut off the alarm clock, and go the fuck back to sleep.

Who the fuck's gonna tell you otherwise?

After all, you're your own boss.

Listen. When you become financially independent, the world becomes your oyster; you do whatever the hell you please. Warren Buffett once said this: "I got half the capital I started with by delivering newspapers. I must have had 20 different [income streams] by the time I left high school."

So get with the program, y'all! Increase your work income—like Warren Buffett did—so that you can maximize your savings. It's the only way.

So, speaking of savings, let's move on to step 2 in our game plan.

STEP 2: SAVINGS

Once you've secured a work income that can cover your monthly expenses, as well as support your savings goal of $300 per week, the next order of business is to, well, save the fucking money.

This is where the savings account I spoke about in *Chapter 2: The Budget* comes into play. If you haven't already, you need to go open a savings account. Once that's done, you need to go visit the human resources department at your job (or *jobs*). Tell your HR representative to automatically wire—from your weekly or biweekly paychecks—the appropriate amount of money into your savings account. Make sure that the money being wired into your savings account averages to $300, or more, per week.

Automatic deposits into your savings account are the best way to go, because it takes the discipline out of the work.

But, alas, your discipline will be challenged in another way.

If you save $300 per week faithfully, after one year, you'll have about $15,600 in your account. That's no small money, people. That's five figures. And now that you have the cash, you'll be tempted to spend it. Not all of it, of course; just a teeny, weeny, tiny bit of it. Your brain will have the following conversation with you: *Why not take a little bit of the money in that huge savings account of yours and book a relaxing vacation to Jamaica. You deserve it, after all. You've been working, slaving, and saving. If anyone deserves a little break, it's you. And, what's the big deal anyway? Taking $3,000 out of the $16,000 you've got saved ain't gonna hurt no one. It's not like you're depleting the entire account. And plus, you're still saving money every week. You'll replenish the account in no time. Come on, let's take the wife and kids and go to Jamaica for a week.*

As humans, we are hardwired to spend money. Cash comes into, and flies out of, our hands like a wild bird. Well, let me tell you guys something: If you're going to be successful at this millionaire challenge, you must keep the bird (your money) in the cage (your savings account). Don't give into any temptations, whatsoever, that require you to spend your savings.

Let me repeat: **Don't... spend... any... of... the... money... in... your... savings... account**!

Period!

Got it?

Good.

Okay. So, you're working hard and earning a suitable income, and you're power-saving that income and refraining from spending any of the money in your savings account.

So, what's next?

I'll tell you: You can save and save all you want, but until you invest your savings in profitable business ventures, you will never experience the exponential growth that is necessary to get you to a million dollars in nine years or less.

So, let's talk a bit about step 3: investments.

STEP 3: INVESTMENTS

Rich people usually invest their savings in 3 places: a tangible business venture; real estate; or the stock market. All three places are great avenues to wealth. But the stock market is by far the quickest and easiest way to multiply your money and achieve financial independence.

You don't believe me?

Well, let's see what our role model Warren Buffett has to say about it. Here's a short excerpt from our favorite book, *Buffett: The Making of an American Capitalist*:

> When a friend suggested that Buffett try his hand in real estate, Buffet grinned. "Why should I buy real estate when the stock market is so easy?" [Buffett exclaimed]."

So, there you have it. If you have the knowledge and the patience, there is no easier way to flip your money than the stock market.

But I am not going to expound on the stock market in this section, though, as we will be discussing the topic at greater length in the following chapter, *Chapter 4: The Stock Market and The Value Investor*. What I *do* want to emphasize, here, is that you need to prepare your mind, starting now, for the time when you will have to invest.

Investments are the reason you are working and saving so hard. I'll put it simply: if you don't invest, you'll never become a millionaire in nine years or less (unless you have an extremely high-paying job). It's virtually impossible. If you simply tried to work and save your way to $1 million, it would take you between 50-70 years to achieve that coveted millionaire status, if not more.

And who the hell wants to wait that long?

I certainly didn't.

And neither should you!

Never forget this powerful quote: *The poor and middle-class work for money, while the rich make their money work for them.*

By putting your money in a stock market portfolio, you are giving it a chance to increase on its own (hopefully exponentially), without you having to lift a single finger.

So, remember, investments are the end goal.

But not just *any* kind of investments.

There are many kinds of stock market investing strategies, the majority of which do not work. *I* will be teaching you an investment strategy called *value investing*. It is the same strategy that Warren Buffett used to turn his thousands into millions, and his millions into billions. We will talk about value investing at length in the next chapter.

Chapter Recap

So, to recap. The Game Plan works. Warren Buffett used it. I used it. And scores of millionaires and billionaires around the world have used it to achieve tremendous wealth. The Game Plan has three steps:

- ***Step 1***: Increase your work income to a level that allows you to pay for your living expenses *and* save $300 per week.
- ***Step 2***: Open a savings account and deposit the $300 per week into it; do this for three years, without ever removing a single penny out of the account, and at the end of three years, you should have roughly $46,800 saved up.
- ***Step 3***: Invest the $46,800 in the stock market for another six years, using the value investing strategy; and at the end of six years, your initial savings will have turned into a one-million-dollar stock portfolio.

Got it?

Cool.

Now, let's move on to the next chapter, where we will discuss how to use the stock market and the value investing approach to multiply the cash you worked so hard to save.

CHAPTER 4

THE STOCK MARKET & THE VALUE INVESTOR!

Dictionary.com defines the stock market as: "a particular market where stocks and bonds are traded."[17]

A stock is a type of security that signifies ownership in a company and represents a claim on part of the company's assets and earnings.

A bond is a debt investment, whereby an investor loans money to a company, which borrows the money for a specific amount of time at a variable or fixed interest rate.

So, essentially, the stock market gives you access to stocks and bonds issued by publicly traded companies. When a company whose stock or bond you own does well, you share in the profits. Just the same, when a corporation whose stock or bond you own doesn't do well, you experience some losses.

It's about timing, pretty much. If you buy the stock of a company at the right time, you'll make a lot of dough. And if, alternatively, you buy the stock of a company at the wrong time, you'll probably lose your shirt.

[17] http://www.dictionary.com/browse/stock-market?s=t

So, James, you may be thinking, *when is the right time to buy a company's stock, so I can get super-rich, real fast, like the man himself, Warren Buffett?*

Well, let me give you a scenario that might explain how you might go about taking advantage of the stock market, in order to generate profitable returns.

Think of the stock market as a huge department store, like Walmart or Target. And the stocks and bonds you buy on the stock market are like the products lining the shelves of that department store.

At our department store, you can buy merchandise and return it at a later date (like anywhere else). But, *unlike* other stores, at our department store, there is no time limit on the return policy. Which means that you can return the stuff you bought whenever you want. As long as the store is open—our department store's hours of business are usually 9:30 AM – 4:00 PM—the store will always accept your returned items.

But there is a little caveat: At our store, when you return an item, you are apt to get a refund that is the same, more, or *less* than what you originally paid for the item. And it is the *store* that determines the return price.

So, as you walk down the isle of our store, you notice that there are two types of shoppers. The first type of shopper is the inexperienced shopper, who buys products at ridiculously high prices. This shopper then gets pissed off when he or she returns the item, and the store refuses to pay him or her an amount that is equal to, or more, than the high price they originally paid. Usually, this kind of shopper ends up having to sell the product back to the store at a price that is lower than what they originally paid for it. And so, this type of shopper always loses money on their store deals.

Then there's a second category of shopper. He or she is an experienced shopper. This type of shopper scans the shelves of our department store, looking for products that are on sale, and which are selling at a major discount to what the product is actually worth. This kind of shopper, for example, will buy a $2.00 pound of turkey, but only when the turkey is on sale for $1.00. Then the shopper will return to the store a few days later, when the sale is over, and sell the turkey back to the store for $2.00. Thus, the experienced shopper made a $1.00 profit on their store deal, which is a 100% return on their original purchase/investment.

In addition to these two types of shoppers, you notice something else—a peculiar trend. The trend is that: Products *rarely* ever go on sale at our department store. In fact, most of the products in the store are *always* overpriced.

And that's when you finally realize what separates the first category of shopper (the inexperienced shopper), from the second type of shopper (the experienced shopper). It all comes down to one word: *Patience.* The experienced shopper is willing to wait for the sales, no matter how long it takes. Whereas the inexperienced shopper isn't. The inexperienced, impulsive shopper has no self-restraint at all; he or she visits the store everyday—sale or no sale—and fills their shopping carts with overpriced items that they have a hard time redeeming at a profit.

So, my question to you, intelligent reader, is: Who is the smarter shopper?

I think we all know the answer to that question. It's obviously our experienced, sale-seeking shopper.

Investopedia.com defines value investing as: "an investment strategy where stocks are selected that trade for less than their intrinsic values."[18] And the same site defines value investors as: "[stock market] investors [who] actively seek stocks they believe the market has undervalued."[19]

Listen folks. There are two types of investors: value investors and speculators.

Speculators buy stocks on a whim, at whatever prices, without knowing the *true* value of the stock they are buying. And when you don't know the true value of something you're buying, it's impossible to know if you're overpaying for it or not.

Value investors, on the other hand, do their homework and find out, first, what the value of the stock they want to buy is. Then, when they know what the value of the stock is, they either buy it (or *don't* buy it) depending on whether or not they can get the stock at a discount price. What's more, value investors understand that stocks, like any other products, rarely go on sale; so, a value investor must exercise a lot of patience as he/she waits for the stock of their choice to go down in price. And only when that stock goes on sale (meaning, when the stock is selling at a discount to its true value), will the value investor buy it.

So, in our "department store" scenario above, it is plain to see that the inexperienced, impulsive shopper is a speculator, while the experienced shopper exhibits the traits of a true value investor.

[18]http://www.investopedia.com/terms/v/valueinvesting.asp?ad=dirN&qo=investopediaSiteSearch &qsrc=0&o=40186

[19]http://www.investopedia.com/terms/v/valueinvesting.asp?ad=dirN&qo=investopediaSiteSearch &qsrc=0&o=40186

You see, companies put shares of their business out on the stock market for people to buy and sell. When you buy a share of a company on the stock market, you own a piece of that company. You can buy as much, or as little, of a company's shares as you want. And the value of the shares you buy will sometimes go up and sometimes go down. When the market price of the stocks you bought rises to an amount that is higher than what you originally paid for them, you can sell the shares on the stock market and make a profit. But if the market price of the stocks you bought drops to an amount that is lower than what you originally paid for them, and you sell the shares, you will lose money.

It's sort of like buying a house. If you buy a house for $300,000, and the market value of similar homes in your neighborhood goes up to $500,000, and you sell your house, you can make a profit of $200,000 on the sale of your home. But if you buy a house for $300,000, and the market value of similar homes in your neighborhood is around $200,000, and you sell your home, you will *lose* $100,000 upon selling.

What the value investing strategy does is teach you how to pinpoint the *true* value of a stock (regardless of what the market price is), so that you can buy that stock when it's selling for less than its true value. When you do that, you give yourself a better chance of getting rich, because oftentimes, if you buy stock in a good company, it's market price will eventually go up to reflect that true value. And when a stock that you bought for less goes up, you make a profit.

But if you buy a stock when it is already selling at a price that is higher than its true value, then you are taking a risk, because once the rest of the investing public realizes what the true value of the stock is (and they always do, eventually), its price will go down in accordance with that value, and then you end up losing money.

So, in the stock market, remember this one rule: buy low, sell high. If you do the opposite (meaning, if you buy high and sell low), you'll always lose money, and you'll go broke in the blink of an eye.

The value investing strategy gives you a precise, mathematically-sound set of criteria that you can use to identify a stock's true value, that way you know whether or not you're overpaying for it. These criteria are what Warren Buffett used to turn a savings nest of $95,000 (adjusted for inflation) into over $65 billion. I will reveal these criteria in *Chapter 6: The Twelve Criteria*. But for now, let me expound a bit more on the stock market.

How do I invest in the stock market? you may be wondering. Is the stock market a physical market place that I have to drive to in order to place my orders?

No. The stock market is not a physical marketplace, per se. While there *is* an actual, physical building in New York City called the New York Stock Exchange, where certain specialists transact in the buying and selling of shares on behalf of third parties, for the most part, the majority of the investing public (which includes institutions, as well as individual investors like yourself), usually invest via a trading platform, which can be found online.

Companies like Scottrade.com, TDAmeritrade.com, and ETRADE.com are called online brokerages. If you want to invest in the stock market, all you have to do is open an account with one of these online brokerage firms. It's similar to opening a regular bank account. Once you're done opening your online brokerage account, the next step is to fund that account. All online brokerage firms will give you the option of wiring money from your personal bank account, into your investment account. And then once you've done that, you can begin buying and selling companies' stocks on the stock market, through your brokerage's website.

Online brokerage firms also supply you with a ton of information on companies' financial status. You can access this valuable information on the firm's website. And you can use this information to help you make smarter decisions about which companies' stocks to buy, sell, or avoid.

We will discuss how to open an online brokerage account in more detail in *Chapter 8: The Brokerage Account*. But for now, let's explore what Warren Buffett's approach to stock market investing was at the start of his career. Let's see whether or not his approach is analogous to the value investing approach we will be using to turn your savings to $1 million.

How Did Warren Buffet Succeed?

A man by the name of Benjamin Graham discovered the value investing approach. Ben Graham was a very successful money manager in the 1940s and 1950s. He was also a professor at Columbia University. Graham taught courses in finance and investing at Columbia. Warren Buffett attended Columbia

University and was a student of Ben Graham's. Everything Warren Buffett knows about investing he learned from Graham. Here are a few excerpts from *Buffett: The Making of An American Capitalist.* These quotes highlight Warren Buffet's investing approach, as taught to him by the father of value investing, Benjamin Graham:

> Graham... urged that investors pay attention not to the [market price], but to the businesses beneath the stock certificates. By focusing on the [business'] earnings, assets, future prospects, and so forth, one could arrive at a notion of a company's intrinsic value that was independent of its market price.
>
> The trick was to invest when prices were far below intrinsic value, and to trust in the market's tendency to correct.
>
> One did not need exactitude—only the skill to identify the occasional company that was priced well below its value.
>
> Buffett was fanatical about following in Graham's footsteps. He invested in stocks held by Graham-Newman Corp., Graham's investment company...
>
> They [Buffett and his classmates] found the Graham strategy—in a nutshell, trying to buy $1 worth of stocks for fifty cents—powerful and absurdly simple, whereas most of Wall Street seemed like shooting craps.
>
> What was most unusual about [Warren] was his appetite for research. Searching for ideas, he read the... Moody's manual [a directory filled with companies' financial information] page for page with the zest of a small boy reading comics. And he found small gems... unwanted and very cheap stocks... [If] the stocks were so cheap, Buffett figured, *somebody* ought to be buying them. But slowly, it dawned on him. That somebody was him. Nobody was going to *tell* you that [a stock] was [cheap]; you had to get there on your own [by doing your own research].

> [Warren once said] "I will tell you the secret of getting rich on Wall Street. Close the doors. You try to be greedy when others are fearful [meaning, buy stocks during market panics, when everybody else is selling, thereby making the price of stocks cheaper] and you try to be very fearful when others are greedy [meaning, refrain from buying stocks during bull markets, when everybody else is buying, thereby making the price of stocks more expensive]."

> Graham's favorite was to hunt for stocks that traded at one-third less than their net working capital—in other words, stocks that were *insanely* cheap. When Buffett [who at this point in time was working as a stock broker at Graham-Newman Corporation] found a stock, he would take it to Graham... And Graham would decide on the spot whether to buy it. It wasn't a matter of *persuading* Graham. A stock either met his criteria or it didn't. He did it by the numbers.

> [Warren] seemed to be bursting to create Graham's entire [achievements].

> Buffett... found a [stock that] was trading at 45 and had $120 a share in cash alone.

> ... the basis for Buffett's career. Stocks would rise to value; therefore, an investor [who bought stocks at a discount, and] who trusted his judgement could be patient.

So how did Warren Buffett succeed?

Well, firstly, he researched the stock market for companies to buy. And when he found a stock that he liked, he determined what its true value was. To effectively do this, Warren analyzed companies' income statements and balance sheets (which I will show you how to do in chapter 5). He also used a set of well-defined criteria to determine whether the company was in good financial standing (which I will show you how to do in Chapter 6). Then, Warren would look at the market price, to see what the investing public was quoting the stock for. If the stock's market price reflected a discount to the stock's true value (and if the company in question was in good financial standing and possessed a strong track-record of profitability), Warren would buy it. But, on the contrary, if the market quoted the stock at a price that was higher than what it was worth (regardless of how profitable the company was) Warren would not purchase it.

Simply put: Warren Buffett became rich by buying shares of *good* companies when they were on *sale*.

Humans are hardwired to gamble. As a result, the majority of the investing public has turned the stock market into a giant casino. People buy stocks at whatever prices—regardless of that stocks' *true* valuation—in the hopes of merely selling it a few days later at a higher price. Everyone's all about the quick buck.

But oftentimes, like in a casino, instead of making a quick buck, they lose their shirts.

The value investing strategy that you will be implementing is not that of a gambler's. In fact, it is a mathematical equation. An algorithm of sorts. It will teach you how to precisely value a company's stock. By knowing exactly what a stock is worth, you will never overpay for another share again.

As you peruse the stock market, you will encounter several stocks that you like. The desire to buy them will be great. But you must let your rationale prevail. You must be patient—like Warren Buffet was. You must wait until the market price of the stock drops beneath its true value, before buying it. And if, after purchasing the stock at a discount, the market price continues to tumble downwards, you must again exercise patience, and refrain from selling. You must trust in your initial judgement and hold on to your stock purchase. And you mustn't sell it, until the market reprices it at, or above, true value.

Patience. Patience. Patience.

That's the name of the game for a value investor.

CHAPTER RECAP

So, to recap.

The stock market is a place, located on the World Wide Web, where shares of companies are bought and sold. Each stock has a market price and a true value. The current market price of that stock may or may not reflect the stock's true value. As a value investor, your job is to, first, figure out what the true value of the stock you're interested in buying is. Once you've figured that out, it is then your duty to never overpay for that stock. You must wait until the market price of the stock drops below its true valuation. Then, and only then, should you purchase it.

Remember: Buy low, sell high.

Never the other way around.

So, now that you know how the stock market works, and now that you understand the concept of never overpaying for a stock, let's move onto the next chapter. In the following chapter, we will discuss the importance of two financial documents. They are the income statement and the balance sheet. They are the tools that you will need to use to accurately determine the true value of a company's stock.

Shall we?

CHAPTER 5

THE INCOME STATEMENT & BALANCE SHEET!

All of a company's financial data can be found on their income statement and balance sheet. All publicly-traded companies on the stock market are required, by the government, to disclose their income statements and balance sheets to the investing public.

"*Why are these documents so important, James*?" you might be wondering.

Well, these documents are extremely important, because the information they contain will help you determine what the true value of a company's stock is. And, as I stressed in the previous chapter, you are only gambling when you buy a stock without knowing it's true value.

And gamblers almost always lose.

But you're not a loser. You're a winner. And stock market winners—like Warren Buffett—win because they do their homework before buying a stock. And that homework consists of analyzing companies' income statements and balance sheets, which are disclosed in a company's annual report.

Don't believe me?

OK, here's what Warren Buffett did to become a successful stock picker.

HOW DID WARREN BUFFET SUCCEED?

Here are some excerpts from our favorite book *Buffett: The Making of an American Capitalist*:

> Buffett spent the day reading annual reports..."
>
> In the evenings... He would go home and read a stack of annual reports. For anyone else it would have been work. For Buffett it was a night on the town.
>
> Buffett can see [the nosy tourists] from his kitchen, where he might be scooping out some ice cream, or grabbing a Cherry Coke to take to his 'pit' to settle in with papers and annual reports.
>
> Buffett told Jack about his own career, recounting his rise as an investor. Jack asked [Buffett], "How do you do it [meaning, how do you invest so well]?" Buffet said he read "a couple of thousand" financial statements [meaning, annual reports] a year.
>
> Buffet became a personal tutor to [Mrs.] Graham [CEO of the Washington Post]. When he came to Washington, he would bring a stack of annual reports and take her through them, line by line.
>
> "Warren wanted annual reports..." Peters noted. Buffet was most annoyed because Peters [a manager who worked at one of Buffett's subsidiaries] didn't produce an annual report. Even in a venture that couldn't possibly make a buck, [Warren] needed that yardstick.

So how did Warren Buffett succeed?

He *prioritized* annual reports, that is what he did.

As stated in the last quote, Warren used annual reports as his "yardstick." Sure, you can measure the length of anything with anything; but using an actual ruler (or other precise measuring apparatus) removes all doubt. Using a ruler provides you with an exact—instead of approximate—measurement of whatever it is you're trying to gauge.

That is what the annual report does. It provides you with the information that allows you to calculate *exactly* what a company is worth. And when you know exactly what a company is worth, as a whole, you can then determine what each individual stock is worth.

A lot of "experts" on TV make inferences regarding what a company *might* be worth. Or what a company is *almost* worth. Or what a company *used* to be worth. These are all guesstimates. And who in the hell wants to rely on a guesstimate? Especially when your hard-earned money is at stake? Not me. What I desire is exactitude. And so should you.

And that is what the annual report (which contains the income statement and balance sheet) will do for you. It will provide you not with a guesstimate, but rather, with the *exact* price that you should be paying for a stock.

OK. Now that you understand how important an annual report is to your investment decision, let's discuss its components (the income statement and balance sheet) at length.

THE INCOME STATEMENT

The first document in the annual report is the income statement. Merriam-Webster defines the income statement as: "a financial statement of a business showing the details of revenues, costs, expenses, losses, and profits for a given period."

Would you want to invest in a company that operates at a loss every year? The obvious answer is no. So why then do institutional investors, big-time hedge funds, and the investing public at large invest in such companies all the time?

Because they're stupid, that's why.

And it is this type of large-scale stupidity that leads to cataclysmic market crashes. I mean, it ain't rocket science. When millions of people are investing in bad assets, what do you *think* is going to happen, eventually?

But you're not stupid.

You're a value investor now. And like Warren Buffett, you spend your time analyzing a company's income statement. Because an income statement tells you how much a company earned for the year, and how much they spent in that same year. And if you subtract that company's expenses from its earnings, you're left with the company's annual *profit margin.*

So, tell me. If you analyze a company's income statement and notice that it is not profitable, should you still invest in that company? The answer to that question is a big fat **NO**!

So, no matter how much you like a company's products or services, if that company does not have a long-standing record of huge annual profits, you should not invest a single penny of your money in them.

If I make $100,000 a year, but I spend $200,000 a year (which puts me in debt $100,000 every year), and I ask you to lend me $10,000, would you give me your hard-earned money? I would like to think that, under those circumstances, you would tell me to kiss your ass. Why? Well, because you're smart enough to know that lending to someone who is severely in debt is not a safe bet.

So why then would you invest your money in a company like Navistar, Inc. (whose ticker symbol is NAV)? If we take a look at Navistar's income statement, we see that in the year 2015, the company earned $1.48 billion dollars. And you might be thinking, *Wow! That's awesome. The company earned more than a billion dollars*! But wait! If we add up all of Navistar's expenses for that same year, it totaled around $1.66 billion dollars. So let's do the math: $1.48 billion - $1.66 billion = - $187 million. Which means that in the year 2015, Navistar didn't make any money at all. In fact, they *lost* $187,000,000. Yet, as I am writing this, their stock is selling for a robust $26.53 per share. Which gives the company an overall market cap (or, market value) of $2.13 billion.

But you want to know what's worst? If we take a closer look at Navistar's income statement, dating back some time, we can see that the company has repeatedly lost money for the past four years. Heck, in the year 2012 alone, they somehow managed to lose $3 billion. This is a horrendous trend, because it shows that the company does not know how to either manage their expenses, increase their revenue, and/or both.

Now, knowing all of this, why would *anyone* invest their money in such a company?

I'll tell you why? Because they *don't* know these statistics. And they *don't* know these stats because they haven't done their homework. They neglected to analyze the company's annual income statements.

But that is a mistake that *you*, as a value investor, will never make. Because *you* will always do your homework before investing in a company. And doing your homework entails studying a company's income statement.

We use the income statement because it reveals how much money a company earned and spent over a certain period of time. And as a result, we are able to determine what the company's profit margins were over the course of that time. An intelligent investor only invests in companies that have robust profit margins (as opposed to robust market prices). And a smart investor also makes sure that these profit margins are consistent, year in and year out, rain, sleet, or snow. That is why it is prudent to analyze a company's income statements dating back as far as you can go. Don't be fooled by companies that show off their stellar single-year profits. Any company can have a wonderful year. But only the truly wonderful companies can sustain that top-notch profitability, year in and year out.

So, let's go back to our earlier lending scenario. If I, on the contrary, make $100,000 a year, and I only spend $20,000 (which leaves me with a profit margin of $80,000 per year), and I ask you to borrow $10,000 at interest, would you lend me the money? The answer in this case is probably yes. Why? Well, because you're smart. And if, after checking my bank account, you confirm that I am in fact making a profit of $80,000 every year, and have sustained this trend for, say, the past five years, you can then make the assumption that I am a very frugal individual. And a very good money manager as well. Thus, lending me your $10,000 is probably a safe bet.

Which is why you'd be better off investing your money in a company like Berkshire Hathaway, Inc.—which happens to be our guy, Warren Buffett's, company.

If we take a look at Berkshire's income statement for the year 2015, we can see that the company earned $52.8 billion dollars. And if we add up all of the company's expenses for that same year, it totals about $28.8 billion. So let's do the math: $58.8 billion - $28.8 billion = $24 billion. Which gives you a profit margin of about 46% ($24 billion of net profit divided by $52.8 billion in total earnings equals .46). You should only invest in companies that have an annual profit margin of 10% or higher. So, when you see a profit margin like Berkshire Hathaway's, that should turn you on, baby.

Furthermore, if we take a closer look at Berkshire's income statements dating back some time, we can see that the company has steadily increased its profit margin every year, for the past five years. Which is a fabulous trend, because it shows us that the company gets a little better, each year, at increasing its income and lowering its costs.

And that is what great businesses do.

When a company is able to budget their expenses to the point where they have lots of money left over at the end of the fiscal year, it shows us that the people managing that company are responsible individuals. But, when a company spends so recklessly that they are left with nothing at the end of the year (like in our Navistar, Inc. example above), that means that the people running the business are incompetent or irresponsible. Or both.

So let me ask you this? As an investor, who would you rather entrust your hard-earned money to? Would you rather hand your cash over to a brain-dead CEO, who is running a company that has a history of reckless spending habits and mounting debt? Or would you rather entrust your dough to the managers of a company with a long history of profitability and strong economic fundamentals?

Because, essentially, that is what you're doing when you invest. You are entrusting your money to the managers of the company you're investing in. And that's why the income statement is so important. Men lie and women lie. But numbers (unless they're cooked), don't lie. So the next time the CEO, or managers, of a company tell you that their company is profitable and, therefore, a safe investment, all you have to do is glance at said company's income statement. Only then will you be able to form your own, educated conclusion as to whether or not the company is actually making money.

Another piece of important data we get from the income statement is something called "diluted shares outstanding." Diluted shares outstanding is basically the number of shares that are currently out on the market, and which are owned by investors (both individual and institutional shareholders).

Why is this number important, James? you may be wondering.

Well, it's important, because when you divide this number into another number located on the balance sheet, called "total equity" (which we will discuss in a bit), what you get is the *actual* true value of the company, on a per-share basis. That way, you'll be able to know what each stock is *truly* worth, regardless of its market price.

Here's how the math looks: Total Equity / Diluted Shares Outstanding = Stock's True Value (on a per-share basis).

And remember, as value investors, we *never* buy a stock when it's selling above its true value.

Right?

Right!

Don't worry. I will show you exactly where to locate the "diluted shares outstanding" number on an income statement, in a later chapter (*Chapter 7: The Sources*). For now, all you need to understand are the reasons why the income statement is so important. The first reason the income statement is important is because it provides us with a company's earnings and expense data. And from this information, we are able to figure out how profitable (or not profitable) a company truly is. We determine this by subtracting annual expenses from annual revenue.

The second reason the income statement is so important is because it provides us with a magic number called "diluted shares outstanding." This number is the total amount of a company's shares that exist on the market, and which are owned by individual and institutional investors. This number is vital because when we divide it into another magic number called "total equity" (which can be found on the balance sheet), we come up with the stock's *true value* (irrespective of its market price).

Capisce, paisan?

Good!

Now that you understand why the income statement is so important, let's discuss the significance of the balance sheet.

THE BALANCE SHEET

The second document in the annual report is the balance sheet. A balance sheet is a statement that shows the financial condition of a company at a particular time, by listing the amount of money and property the company owns, along with the amount of debt the company owes.

So, while the income statement shows us how much a company earns and spends on an annual basis, the balance sheet reveals how many assets a company possesses, as well as how much debt a company owes, in total.

As you probably already know, when you subtract someone's total debt from the total value of his/her assets, you get… bingo!... the person's net worth. Here's how the math looks: Total Assets – Total Debt = Net Worth.

Well, the same concept is used to figure out a company's net worth. If you take all of a company's assets, and subtract all of a company's debt from those assets, you'll be left with the company's net worth, which is also called the company's "total equity."

This term should ring a bell, as we discussed it briefly in the previous section about the income statement. "Total equity" is one of the two magic numbers (the other being "diluted shares outstanding") that we use to determine the net worth (or true value) of a company's individual stock. In *Chapter 7: The Resources*, I'll show you exactly where to find the "total equity" number on a balance sheet, as well as the "diluted shares outstanding" number on an income statement. That way, you will be able to calculate exactly what a share of a company is truly worth. But for now, just remember that the balance sheet reveals, in total, what a company owns (by way of assets), and what a company owes (by way of debt).

Let's discuss the importance of a balance sheet further by using an example.

I ask you to lend me $10,000. And you, being the smart value investor that you are, ask to see my balance sheet. So, I have my accountant prepare the balance sheet and send it over to you.

Now, when you get the balance sheet, you notice that I possess about $300,000 worth of assets (taking into account the value of my home, my car, the cash I have on hand, and a few other possessions). But then you take a look at the debt side of my balance sheet, and you notice that I *owe* $1,000,000 (mostly to banks and credit card companies).

So, what is my net worth?

Well, let's do the math. $300,000 (assets) - $1,000,000 (debt) = - $700,000 (net worth).

So, as we can see in the above example, I *owe* more than I *own*, which actually gives me a *negative* net worth. I am severely in debt, which means that I am probably terrible at managing my own money.

So, knowing this, are you still willing to lend me yours?

I didn't think so.

Well, the same principle applies for analyzing companies on the stock market.

Millions of people invest their money daily in this or that company, without taking into account the company's financial standing. A lot of these companies are financially broke. Literally. And if an investor took a second to glance at the company's balance sheet, he or she would know that. But out of sheer laziness, or stupidity, or negligence, or whatever, the public *doesn't* do their homework. Instead, they base their investment decisions on what slick-talking financial "experts" on TV tell them. Or, they listen to friends and family who have no knowledge of the markets whatsoever.

Take Avon Products, Inc., for example (whose ticker symbol on the stock market is AVP). Avon is a big cosmetics manufacturer with a market cap of $2.29 billion. As I am writing this, if we take a look at Avon's balance sheet, we can see that Avon owns $3.8 billion in assets, but owes $4.9 billion in debt. When we subtract the debt from the assets, the value of the company, as a whole, stands at - $1.1 billion. Which means that this company actually has a *negative* valuation. Its stock is worth zero dollars—actually, roughly one billion dollars *less* than zero dollars.

Yet, as I am writing this, Avon's shares are selling on the stock market for $5 a pop. Which means, people are actually buying AVP shares, and thus the reason for its multi-billion-dollar market cap.

(*Smh*).

But you'll never be one of those people. Not anymore.

You're a value investor now. And value investors do their homework before buying stocks.

Okay. New example.

John Smith asks you to lend him $10,000. And you, being the smart, value investor that you are, ask to see his balance sheet. So, he has his accountant prepare the balance sheet document and send it over to you. When you take a look at his balance sheet, you notice that Mr. Smith possesses about $1,000,000 worth of assets (taking into account the value of his home, his car, the cash he has in the bank, and some other valuable possessions). And when you take a look at the debt side of his balance sheet, you notice that he owes only $10,000 (mostly to student loan companies—which means that Mr. Smith has no consumer debt).

So, what is John Smith's net worth?

Well, let's do the math. $1,000,000 (assets) - $10,000 (debt) = $990,000 (net worth).

So, in this new example, it is obviously clear that Mr. John Smith *owns* more than he *owes*. In fact, Mr. Smith has been so thrifty over the years, that he has accumulated a robust net worth of nearly $1 million. This surplus of assets over debt shows that Mr. Smith is very good at managing his money and finances.

So, in this scenario, would you be more willing to lend your hard-earned $10,000 to Mr. Smith?

Heck yeah!

Well, the same principle applies when it comes to investing your money in the stock market.

Let's take Travelers Companies, Inc. for example (whose ticker symbol on the stock market is TRV). They're a huge insurance provider.

At the time of this writing, if we take a look at Travelers balance sheet, we notice that the company owns $101.96 billion in assets, and owes $78.36 billion in debt. When we subtract the debt from the assets, the value of the company, as a whole, stands at $23.6 billion. Which means that the company has a positive valuation. This tells us that the managers of Travelers are running the organization in a manner that has grown their asset-base over the years, while keeping debt at a manageable level. And what's more, if we take a closer look at Travelers balance sheet, we notice that this positive valuation has been consistently maintained over the course of the past five years. Which means that good money management at Travelers Companies Inc. is the rule, not the exception.

So, although you may like Avon's cosmetic products more than you do Traveler's insurances packages, I'd like to think that, as a fundamentally sound value investor, you'd be more inclined to entrust your heard-earned capital with the managers running Travelers. Why? Well, because they've proven that they have a long track record of maintaining high levels of profitability. *That's* why!

Another piece of important data we can glean from the balance sheet is something called "total equity." Total equity is basically the number you get after you subtract a company's total debt from it total assets. "Total equity" is essentially the company's net worth, as a whole.

Why is this number so important, James? you might be wondering.

Well, as aforementioned, it's important because when you divide the "total equity" number by the "diluted shares outstanding" number (which we mentioned in the previous section, on the income statement), you come up with a figure that represents exactly what each individual stock of a company is *truly* worth, irrespective of its market price.

So, here's how the math looks: Total Equity / Dilute Shares Outstanding = Stock's True Value (on a per-share basis).

So, let's use Travelers Companies Inc. as an example. At present, the company's "total equity" is $23.6 billion. And the company has 313.9 million "diluted shares outstanding" on the market. So, if we divide $23.6 billion by 313.9 million shares, we get $75.18. That is the true value of each individual

Travelers, Inc. stock. Here's the math again: $23,600,000,000 (total equity) / 313,900,000 (diluted shares outstanding) = $75.18 (each stock's true value).

So, as I am writing this, each stock of TRV (Travelers) is truly worth $75.18.

Not a penny more.

Remember now, as value investors, we never buy a stock when it's selling at a price that exceeds its true value. So, as I am writing this, TRV stock is currently selling at $109.62 per share on the stock market. Which means that, although Travelers is a wonderful company, run by very capable managers, due to the fact that its stock is selling at a premium to its true value, we cannot buy it.

But that doesn't mean that we can't keep TRV on our radar. Because, let's say, the stock were to go down to $65 per share next quarter. That would mean that the stock was on sale, because, then, it'd be selling for $10 less than what it's truly worth (which is $75.18). And that presents us with a buying opportunity. Because as value investors, we only buy the stocks of wonderful companies when they are selling at a discount to their *true* value.

Chapter Recap

So, let's recap.

The income statement and balance sheet are the two documents—found in a company's annual report—that we use to assess whether or not a company's stock is investable.

The income statement tells you how much a company earns and spends on a quarterly and annual basis. When you subtract a company's expenses from its earnings, you get the company's profit margin for that given period of time. You should only invest in companies that have a long track record of yielding profit margins of 10% or more annually.

The income statement also provides you with a magic number called "diluted shares outstanding." This number represents the amount of a company's stock that is currently available on the open market. This number is important because, when you divide it into another magic number called "total equity" (which can be found on the balance sheet), you come up with the true value of a company's individual stock. And as a value investor, it is critical to discern what a stock's true value is, so that you can know if you are overpaying for the stock or not.

Next, we discussed the balance sheet. The balance sheet is just as important as the income statement. The balance sheet shows us, in aggregate, how much assets a company possesses, and how much debt a company owes. When you subtract a company's debt from its assets, you get the entire company's net worth, as a whole. This is also called the company's "total equity."

"Total equity" is our second magic number (the first being the "diluted shares outstanding" figure, which can be found on the income statement). "Total equity" is an extremely important number because, as we discussed earlier, when you divide "total equity" by "diluted shares outstanding" you get an individual stock's true value. Here's how the math looks: Total Equity / Diluted Shares Outstanding = Stock's Value (on a per-share basis).

In *Chapter 7: The Resources,* I will show you exactly where to find the "diluted shares outstanding" number on the income statement, and where to find the "total equity" number on a balance sheet.

We good so far?

Alrighty then.

Now that you know why the income statement and balance sheet are so important—they supply us with the two magic numbers needed to determine the true value of an individual stock—let's delve into the 12 criteria that will serve as your litmus test, when deciding whether or not to pick a stock for your investment portfolio.

CHAPTER 6

THE 12 CRITERIA!

Alright, my budding investor-entrepreneur.

Now that you know how to use the income statement and balance sheet to calculate what a company's stock is truly worth, we are going to take a look at the 12 overall criteria that must be met before a company's stock can be deemed safe for investment.

Please understand that the more of these criteria a company's stock meets, the less risky the investment, because it means that the company is fundamentally strong and sound. And the inverse is also true; if a stock does not meet a majority (or all) of the 12 criteria, that means that the company is fundamentally weak, thus making an investment in that stock very risky.

Before discussing the 12 criteria, let me reiterate this point, because it is very important. A stock speculator and a value investor are two, totally different people. A speculator places bets on a hunch, without following any clearly defined rules or guidelines, much like a degenerate gambler. And the end result is usually huge errors of judgment that lead to loss of capital.

Whereas a value investor (which you now are—Yah!) operates by using a sound investment strategy. This strategy contains a set of guidelines and criteria that help minimize risk. A value investor minimizes risk by, first, determining a stock's true value, because by knowing the true value of a share, a value investor can guard against overpaying for that stock.

Then, after determining the true value of a stock, a value investor evaluates such things as a company's profitability, liquidity, and debt-load, which paints a precise picture of overall management efficiency. All of these things must be taken into account before a sound investment decision can be made.

So, if you want to be a speculator, go right ahead. You'll get that same rush, that same high, that all gamblers get. But in the end, you'll *lose* all of your money.

But if you actually want to *make* money trading stocks, stick to the value investing strategy, by making sure that the stocks you're targeting for investment meet as much of the following 12 criteria as possible:

1. **True Value**: Make sure that the company's stock is selling at a discount to its *true value* before purchasing it.
2. **Dividend**: Make sure the stock in question pays a dividend of at least 2.5% or more.
3. **ROIC (Return on Invested Capital)**: Make sure that the stock in question possesses a Return on Invested Capital rate of at least 10% or more.
4. **ROE (Return on Equity)**: Make sure that the stock in question possesses a Return on Equity rate of at least 10% or more.
5. **Net Profit Margin**: Make sure that the stock in question possesses a Net Profit Margin rate of at least 10% or more.
6. **P/E Ratio**: Make sure that the stock in question possesses a Price to Earnings ratio of 15 or less.
7. **Price/Sales Ratio**: Make sure that the stock in question possesses a Price to Sales ratio of between 0.6-1.5.
8. **Price/Book Ratio**: Make sure that the stock in question possesses a Price to Book ratio of between 0.6-1.5.
9. **Debt/Equity Ratio**: Make sure that the stock in question possesses a Debt to Equity ratio of .50 or less.
10. **Current Ratio**: Make sure that the stock in question possesses a Current Ratio of at least 1.5 or more.
11. **Quick Ratio**: Make sure that the stock in question possesses a Quick Ratio of at least 1.5 or more.

12. **Trend Numbers: Sales, Earnings Per Share, Book Value Per Share, Free Cash Flow, Working Capital**: Make sure that the company in question possesses a steady and/or growing trend of Sales, Earnings Per Share (or EPS), Book Value Per Share (or BVPS), Free Cash Flow (or FCF), and Working Capital, dating back ten years.

Unless you're an experienced stock market investor, you probably don't know what these terms mean. Don't worry. In a few moments, I will define each term, and explain why it is important to your investment decision. But before I do, I want to be clear on one point. And this is very important, so listen up: You will rarely, if ever, find a stock that meets all 12 criteria.

What the fuck, James?! Why the hell are you wasting my time with these 12 criteria, if I'll never find a stock that fits the bill? you may be pondering.

Well, my friend, because when you reach for the stars, if you miss, at least you will land on the moon. Which beats reaching for the clouds, missing, and landing flat on your ass, on the ground.

A stock that actually meets all of these criteria would be the *perfect* company. And if you've been alive for more than a week, you know that nothing in life is ever perfect. But does that mean we should lower our standards? Of course not. You should always strive for perfection; true, you may never find or achieve it, but, at least you'll come damn close.

What I am saying is, you want to look for stocks that meet as much of these criteria as possible. I don't invest in any stocks that don't, at the very least, satisfy 9 out of the 12 criteria (which is about a 75% approval rating). If I find a stock that satisfies more than 9 out of the 12 criteria, I do a hand-stand. And then I invest a boat-load of money into that stock because its fundamental strengths are off the chart!

The only exception to that rule is when a stock doesn't satisfy Criteria #1 (the True Value criteria), and Criteria # 12 (the Trend Numbers criteria). A stock may satisfy 10 out of the 12 criteria. But if it is overpriced, and if its trend numbers are decreasing or unstable, I will not buy it. And neither should you. What you do at that point is keep that stock on your radar, and follow it closely. And the second its market price dips below its true value, *and* it's trend numbers show massive improvement over the course of a longer period, then you pounce. And pounce heavy.

Okay.

Now, let's quickly define these terms and discuss why they are important to your investment analysis.

1. TRUE VALUE

I think we've exhausted this criterion ad nauseam. But it never hurts to repeat an important point. So, here we go. Again.

You should *never* buy a stock based on its current market price. Why? Well, because the current market price may, or may not, reflect that stock's *true* value. Thus, you should only purchase a stock when it is selling at a discount to its true value.

In order to calculate a stock's true value, you divide its "Total Equity" number (which can be found on the company's balance sheet) by its "Diluted Shares Outstanding" number (which can be found on the company's income statement). That will give you the net worth, or true value, of the stock on a per-share basis.

Only *then* does the market price become relevant.

Why? Well, because if the market price is higher than the true value, then the stock is overpriced, and you should refrain from buying it. No matter how attractive it may be. But if, on the other hand, the market price is *below* the true value, that means that the stock is on sale, and therefore warrants further investigation.

It's really that simple, people.

Buy your stocks like you do your groceries—when they're on sale.

To do otherwise will cost you long-term capital loss, which is the biggest failure a stock-picker can experience.

2. DIVIDEND

You want to make sure that the stock you are thinking about buying shells out a healthy dividend of 2.5% or more.

Some companies—not all—pay you back a percentage of the money you invested, for as long as you own the stock. These payments are called dividends. So, for example, as I am writing this, Annaly Capital Management, a real estate company whose ticker symbol is NLY, is currently paying an annual dividend of 10%. Which means that if I invest $100,000 in NLY stock, they will pay me $10,000 (10%) over the course of the year.

Simply for owning their stock.

Companies usually pay out dividends on a quarterly basis (every three months). But on rare occasions, you'll find companies that make dividend payments on a monthly basis (which is pretty cool).

Companies usually pay dividends because they are running a smooth and profitable operation. And because they are profitable, they always have extra cash lying around. Some of this extra cash they use to reinvest back into the company, in order to improve, or expand, their operations. But the portion of the extra cash that they *don't* use, they pay out to their shareholders, sort of as a "thank you" for being a valued investor.

It's important that a company pay you a dividend. When you invest in the stock market, you're giving a company *your* heard-earned money, so that it can increase its own productivity and profitability. Therefore, when the company generates profits, it's only fair that they share that surplus with you. Be wary of companies that have an overabundance of cash on their balance sheet (which means that they are operating profitably), yet refuse to pay their investors a dividend. The first question to ask is: What are they doing with all of that extra cash? And once you've found the answer to that question, ask yourself another: Is what they're doing with that extra cash improving the company's productivity and/or increasing the company's profitability? Because if the answer to question number two is no, then management is obligated to share those profits with its investors.

Now, something else needs to be said about dividends. Dividends are not always what they're cracked up to be. Some companies use a dividend payment *strictly* to attract investors. And not because their operations are profitable. These kinds of companies usually finance their dividend payments with debt, instead of company profits. So if you see a company with an unusually large dividend pay-out, investigate the company a bit further to see how much debt they are carrying on their balance sheet. Or check the company's debt/equity ratio (which we will discuss under Criteria # 9). If the company has a lot of debt, then their dividend payment should be questioned. Dividend payments can be cut, or discontinued, at any time. So if you come across a company with lots of debt and a huge dividend payout, you can rest assured that those dividend payments won't last for too long. That company is basically using the dividend payment as a mirage, to bait and hook you into buying their stock. And once shit hits the fan, and that company can no longer answer to their debt obligations, they will swiftly discontinue their dividend payments.

Or worst, file for bankruptcy.

But if, on the other hand, the company has little to no debt, then their dividend payments are probably coming from the company's profits, which is fine and dandy. That's what we *want* to see.

Either way, before investing in a company, make sure that it has a long history of paying out at least 2.5% in annual dividends. Because, after all, it *is* your money that is at risk. So, it's only right that you be compensated accordingly.

3. ROIC

Next is Return On Invested Capital (or ROIC). You want to make sure that the company you're investing in has a long track record of yielding an ROIC rate of at least 10% or more per year.

ROIC is basically a measuring tool that is used to assess how efficiently the management of a company is investing the money you give them. ROIC is calculated as a percentage. One way to calculate ROIC is: Net Income (after tax) – Dividends / Total Capital Invested[20].

In Chapter 7, I will show you exactly where to find the ROIC number using the marketwatch.com website. That way you won't have to keep plugging numbers into the formula that I cited above whenever you find a stock you'd like to evaluate.

For now, let's use an example to better explain ROIC. Let's say you buy 1,000 stocks of XYZ Company at $100 per share. That's a total investment of $100,000. The management of XYZ Company will then take your $100,000 and they will do one of two things with it. They will either use your $100,000 irresponsibly and lose a portion, or all, of it. Or, they will invest your money intelligently, and use it to improve XYZ Company's productivity, which will result in the growth in value of your $100,000. This growth is measured in percentage points. So, if, for example, XYZ Company takes your money and uses it to expand one of their product lines, which results in an end-year profit of 15%, then the value of your money just went from $100,000 to $115,000 ($100K Initial Investment + $15K Profit = $115K Total Value).

That should make you smile.

But if a bunch of bozos are managing XYZ Company, and they take your money and use it to buy private jets that don't add any value to the company's bottom line, and at the end of the year the company suffers a 15% loss, then

[20] Investopedia.com: http://www.investopedia.com/terms/r/returnoninvestmentcapital.asp

the value of your $100,000 just dropped to $85,000 ($100K Initial Investment - $15K Loss = $85K Total Value).

And that should piss you the hell off.

That's why you should research a company's financial numbers before you invest in their stock. The ROIC number is a profitability (and management efficiency) gauge. So it's very important that this number be as high as possible, and never less than 10%. If a company's ROIC numbers are in the single digits, walk away. Fuck that, run! Because that means that the company is not operating as profitably as you might have thought.

Again, I will show you exactly where to find this number—as well as all of the other criteria numbers—in the following chapter. So, don't worry. I'm going to make this process as easy as possible for you.

Now that you understand what the ROIC criteria is, and why it is so important to your investment decision, let's move on to the next criteria, Criteria #4: ROE, or, Return on Equity.

4. ROE

Before investing in a company's stock, make sure it has an ROE (or, Return on Equity) rate of 10% or more.

Like the ROIC number, ROE is calculated as a percentage, and also serves as a profitability (and management efficiency) gauge. In essence, ROIC and ROE are siblings.

The only difference is, when calculating ROE, dividend payments and taxes are not subtracted from the net income.

So, here is the formula for calculating ROE: ROE = Net Income (pre-tax and pre-dividends) /Shareholder's Equity.

Again, in Chapter 7, I will show you exactly where to find the ROE number using the marketwatch.com website. That way you don't have to bother fiddling around with the equation cited above.

If you're still confused as to the difference between ROIC and ROE, let me put it more simply. Analyst use ROIC to compare the profitability of companies in different sectors (for example, a fast-food chain company, and a car manufacturing company). Whereas, ROE is used, more so, to compare the profitability of companies that are within the same sector.

So, for example, we would use ROE to do a comparative analysis between McDonald's and Wendy's, since they are in the same industry/sector. But if we wanted to do a comparative analysis between McDonald's and Ford Motor Company (two companies that are in different market sectors), we would use the ROIC metric instead.

So, as I am writing this, if we take a look at McDonald's company profile on marketwatch.com (which I will show you how to do later on), we see that McDonald's—ticker symbol MCD—has an ROE of 45.53. In other words, 45.53%. Conversely, if we take a look at Wendy's company profile—ticker symbol WEN—we notice that Wendy's has an ROE of 11.33, or, 11.33%. Now, while both McDonald's and Wendy's ROEs are above our 10% benchmark, whether or not you prefer eating Wendy's sandwiches over Mickey D's burgers, when it comes to making an investment in one or the other company, the obvious choice here is McDonald's. Why? Well, because McDonald's ROE of 45.3% is more robust than Wendy's 11.3% output.

When you find a company you want to invest in, don't just analyze that company individually. You must compare the company you want to invest in with its competitors (meaning, the other businesses in its sector). Because nothing kills profits like competition.

And *that* is where ROE comes into play.

ROE is a comparison metric for companies within the *same* sector. Whereas, ROIC is a comparison metric for companies in *different* sectors.

So, before you invest in Ford Company stock, for example, analyze other car company's ROE, to see which company is yielding the largest returns within the car manufacturing sector. Typically (though not always), you want to invest in the company whose return on equity is the highest in its market. Because that means that said company has some kind of economic advantage over the rest of its competitors, since its returns out-muster everyone else's.

But if you're trying to decide on whether to invest in McDonald's or Ford Motor Company (two companies that belong to different sectors), you should use the ROIC number, instead of the ROE metric.

Either way, you should *never* invest in companies with ROEs (or ROICs) *under* 10%. Ever!

Capisce?

Good!

Alright, now that we understand the significance of the ROE metric—and how it is slightly different from its sibling, ROIC—let's discuss the next criteria, Criteria #5: Net Profit Margin.

4. NET PROFIT MARGIN

You want to make sure that the company you're investing in has a long track record of yielding a Net Profit Margin rate of at least 10% or more per year.

The net profit margin percentage is important because it shows you how profitable a company *really* is. The amount of sales a company generates, as a whole, is called total revenue. But all companies have costs and expenses too; that's where the term "the cost of doing business" comes from. The net profit margin is merely the percentage of revenue that's left (from the total revenue) after the company has finished paying off all of their bills and expenses. The formulas for calculating net profit margin are as follows:

- Total Revenue – Total Expenses = Net Profit
- Net Profit/ Total Revenue = Net Profit Margin[21].

Confusing?

Ok, I understand.

Well, let me explain it further (and, hopefully, more simply).

ABC Company earns a total revenue of $100,000 for the year. All of its expenses (including cost of goods sold, operating expenses, interest payments, and taxes) come out to $80,000. So, let's plug these numbers into our first formula. Total Revenue ($100,000) – Total Expenses ($80,000) = Net Profit ($20,000).

Now, to turn that $20,000 into a percentage, we use the second formula. So, Net Profit ($20,000) / Total Revenue ($100,000) = Net Profit Margin (0.2 or 20%).

Which means that ABC Company passes our test for this 5th criteria (since we only want to invest in companies with net profit margins of 10% or higher).

For those of you who are more visual, here's how it looks in graph form (which is how it would be laid out on a company's income statement):

[21] http://www.investinganswers.com/financial-dictionary/financial-statement-analysis/net-profit-margin-2233

INCOME STATEMENT FOR ABC COMPANY, INC.

Total Revenue		$100,000
Costs of Goods Sold		**($20,000)**
Gross Profit		**$80,000**
Operating Expenses		
Salaries	$20,000	
Rent	$10,000	
Utilities	$5,000	
Depreciation	$5,000	
Total Operating Expenses		**($40,000)**
Interest Expenses		**($10,000)**
Taxes		**($10,000)**
Net Profit		**$20,000**

As you can see, ABC Company sells $100,000 worth of products and/or services. But no company gets to keep *all* of their revenue. There are costs and expenses that come with running a business. After paying off all of those costs and expenses, ABC Company is left with a net profit of $20,000 (from the $100,000 it originally earned). And $20,000 is 20% of $100,000. Therefore, ABC Company's net profit margin is 20%.

Which is good.

The higher a company's net profit margin, the more efficient it is. There are only two ways to achieve efficiency when running a business:

1. Increase sales
2. Cut costs

Companies that do these two things well usually have very healthy net profit margins. I'll show you exactly where you can find a company's net profit margin information in the next chapter. But for now, just remember that the net profit margin is the money the company gets to keep after it's done paying all of its bills and covering all of its expenses. This number is calculated as a percentage (of total revenue). And the higher this percentage, the more efficient the company is.

And, whatever you do, as a value investor, you must *never* invest in a company whose net profit margins are below 10%. If you do that, you'll be committing financial suicide.

Copacetic?

Cool.

Now, let's move on to the next criteria, Criteria #6: P/E Ratio.

6. P/E RATIO

Make sure that the stock you want to buy possesses a Price to Earnings ratio (or P/E Ratio) of 15 or less.

James, what the fuck is a price to earnings ratio? you might be wondering.

Well, I'm gonna tell you what a P/E Ratio is.

So listen up.

The PE Ratio is a fairly easy concept to understand. It is merely the market price of a company's stock, relative to the annual net income earned by the company. The PE ratio is basically a valuation metric. It shows us whether a stock is overvalued or undervalued.

So, if the PE ratio of XYZ Company is 10, that means that, at the current market price, XYZ Company is selling for ten times more than XYZ Company's *net* earnings.

The formula for deciphering the PE ratio is as follows: Market Price / Earnings Per Share. (We will go over earnings per share a bit later).

As you've probably already guessed, the PE Ratio is a very important number for us as value investors. Namely because we do not want to overpay for a stock. But rarely will you ever find a PE ratio of 0 (which would mean that the market price and the company's earnings are equal). So the next best thing is to find stocks with PE ratio's that are as close to 0 as possible, and *never* over 15. If a stock's PE ratio is over 15, that means that the company is seriously overvalued. If you were to purchase the stocks of such a company, you'd be overpaying for it. And as value investors, in order to decrease risk, and protect our financial upside, we only invest in stocks that are selling at a discount to true value. Because the cheaper the stock is, the higher our margin of safety is.

In the equities market, PE ratios under 15 suggest that the stock is fairly cheap. Most investors know this. Yet, I've seen individual, institutional, and professional investors buy shares of companies with PE ratios in the 40s, 50s, 60s, and even 100s.

Why the fuck would anyone do that? you might be wondering.

Well, because they're stupid, illogical people, that's why.

Hell, would you pay $30 million for a rental property that earns you only $12,000 in rental income per year? The answer is heck no! (Shit, according to those numbers it would take you 2,500 years to make your money back). Yet, people engage in such behavior all of the time when buying and selling stocks. And the reason they do this is because they don't view a stock for what it truly is.

When you buy a stock, you are acquiring a percentage of an actual, tangible business. You're not merely buying blips or flashing numbers on a ticker tape. Warren Buffett has said plenty of times in the past that an investor should treat the purchase of a single share as though he were buying the entire company. So, if a single share of ABC Company is selling for $10, and ABC Company currently has 2 billion shares outstanding, that means that the market is currently valuing ABC Company at $20 billion ($10 per share x 2 billion shares outstanding = $20 billion valuation). So, as a value investor, you should ask yourself the question: Would I be willing to pay $20,000,000,000 for ABC Company? And if the answer to that question is a vehement *no*, then you shouldn't pay $10 for one of its shares either. Because that's what you're doing when you purchase ABC Company at $10 a share. You're essentially paying $20 billion for the company, as a whole.

Now, on the other hand, if you analyze ABC Company's fundamentals and realize that ABC Company is actually worth $40 billion, then buying it at a market price of $20 billion is smart, because now you're buying it at a 50% discount.

So… what am I trying to say here?

Exactly what I've been saying the entire book: Don't *ever* overpay for a stock. And in the equities market, once a stock's PE ratio surpasses 15, it suggests that the stock is overvalued. So, stay the fuck away from it. Only buy stocks with PE ratios under 15. And if you *really* want to acquire a bargain stock, shares with PE ratios in the single digits are the best.

Copacetic?

Good!

Now, let's move onto the next criteria, Criteria # 7: Price to Sales Ratio.

7. PS RATIO

Before investing in a company's stock, make sure it has a Price to Sales Ratio (or PS ratio) between 0.6 and 1.5.

The PS ratio—like the PE ratio—is also a valuation metric. It is merely the market price of a company's stock, relative to the annual sales generated by the company.

The formula for PS ratio is: Market Price / Sales Per Share.

The difference between the PE ratio and the PS ratio is this: PE ratio compares the company's market price to the company's *net* earnings or income (after all expenses have been paid); whereas the PS ratio compares the company's market price to its *total* sales or revenue (that is, *before* interests, taxes, depreciation, and amortization have been paid).

In other words:

1. PE ratio compares market price to *net* earnings.
2. PS ratio compares market price to *gross* sales.

That's it.

If you want a more accurate valuation of the company, using the PE ratio might be your best bet. But that doesn't mean you should ignore the PS ratio. Because it is definitely useful as well.

For example, the PS ratio comes in handy when you consider the fact that sales numbers are a bit harder to manipulate (accounting-wise) than earnings. Tangible receipts back up sales. Whereas, net earnings … well, let's just say that a crafty accountant can manipulate or misrepresent deductions in a way that leaves the final number (meaning, the net income), looking a bit glossier than it truly is. For that reason alone, some people prefer the PS ratio number over the PE ratio number.

But, whichever you prefer (PE or PS ratio), what you should *never* do is buy a stock with a PS ratio beneath 0.6, or over 1.5. If the PS ratio is above 1.5, you're overpaying for the stock if you buy it. And if the PS ratio is under 0.6, it means that the stock is not a fundamentally-sound one, financially speaking, that is.

I will show you exactly where to find the PS ratio number in the next chapter. But for now, just remember the following 4 points we've discussed so far:

1. PE ratio compares market price to *net* earnings.
2. PS ratio compares market price to *gross* sales.
3. Only buy a stock with a PS ratio of between 0.6 - 1.5.

Alright?

Cool.

Now, let's move on to Criteria # 8: Price to Book Ratio.

8. PB RATIO

Before investing in a company's stock, make sure it has a Price to Book Ratio (or PB ratio) between 0.6 and 1.5.

I know, I know.

You have no idea what the hell a PB ratio is.

Well, I'll explain.

The price to book ratio (again, like the PE and PS ratios) is a valuation metric. It is merely the market price of a company's stock, relative to the tangible net worth of the company.

The formula for the PB ratio is: Market Price / Total Assets – Intangible Assets + Liabilities.

The PB ratio is perhaps the most important valuation metric of the 3 we've discussed so far (PE, PS, and PB ratios). It basically tells you how overpriced, or underpriced, the stock truly is.

For example, a PB ratio of 15 means that the market price of that stock is 15 times more than what the company is actually, tangibly worth.

It's really that simple.

I will show you where to find the PB ratio later. But for now, just remember that you should only buy stocks with PB ratios of 0.6 – 1.5.

Oh, and as a small recap:

1. PE ratio compares a company's market price to its *net* earnings.
2. PS ratio compares a company's market price to its *gross* sales.
3. And PB ratio compares a company's market price to its *tangible net worth*.

Ready for more?

Good.

Next up is Criteria #9: Debt to Equity ratio.

9. DE RATIO

Before investing in a company's stock, make sure it has a Debt to Equity Ratio (or DE ratio) below .50 (or 50%).

The DE ratio is also a valuation metric (like the PE, PS, and PB ratios). The DE ratio represents the company's total debt relative to its equity (or, assets—after all liabilities have been accounted for).

So, for example, if a company has $1,000,000 worth of liabilities (or debt), and has a total of $4,000,000 worth of assets (or equity), the math would look something like this: $1,000,000 (total liabilities) / $4,000,000 (shareholder equity) = .25 (or 25%). Which is great because it falls within our parameters, since we want the stocks we invest in to have a DE ratio below 50%.

When a company has a DE ratio of over .50, it means that the company has more debts than assets. Which also means that the company is not being managed very well.

Would you feel comfortable lending your hard-earned money to Person A, who has $5,000 in the bank, but is in debt $100,000; or Person B, who has $100,000 in the bank, and is in debt only $5,000?

I think the choice is clear.

Person B would get your loan.

Yet, stock market investors always make the error of forking over their hard-earned money to companies that have way more debt than assets. Why? Why? Why?

Folly.

Madness.

Stupidity.

That's why.

But you're a value investor now. And value investors are smart. We *think* before we buy our stocks. We analyze the numbers, to make sure that we're investing in a company that is fundamentally sound.

I will show you exactly where to find the DE ratio in the next chapter. But for now remember that you should only invest in companies with DE ratios below .50.

So, if a company's DE ratio is .51 (or 51%), it means that, out of all of the company's equity, 51% is made up of debt, and 49% is made up of assets. Which means that the company has more debt than assets.

In which case you ignore it.

Only invest your money in fundamentally sound businesses. And a company with more debt than its got assets is not fundamentally sound—it's mismanaged. To say the least.

Capisce?

Good.

Let's move right along to our next ratio, Criteria # 10: Current Ratio.

10. CURRENT RATIO

Before investing in a company's stock, make sure it has a Current Ratio of 1.5 or more.

The current ratio is not a valuation metric, but rather a liquidity metric. It measures a company's ability to pay its short-term liabilities (or debts) with its current assets.

The formula is simple: Current Assets (*including* Inventories) / Current Liabilities.

Current liabilities are bills that have to be paid within a year.

Current assets are valuable properties (such as inventories, accounts receivable and other chattel) that the company currently possesses, on hand.

So, for example, if you own $1 million worth of cars, boats, homes and other equitable assets that can be converted to cash quickly, and all of your annual bills total $50,000, the math would look something like this: $1,000,000 (current assets) / $50,000 (current liabilities) = 20. Which means that you have 20 times more current assets than you do current debt (or liabilities).

So, a current ratio of 1.5 or above simply means that a company has 50% or more current assets than current debt. Thus, a company with a current ratio of 2 is one that has 100% (or twice as much) more current assets than current debt. Which, in turn, implicates that the company is being very well-managed.

But what if a company has a current ratio of 1?

Well, that means that the company's current assets and current debts are equal. They're just making it by. Hence, if a catastrophe were to beset that company, they would have no equitable reserves with which to dig themselves out of a hole. So, in essence, they'd be forced to borrow money, which would tip that current ratio below 1, making the company more debt-laden than cash- or asset-rich.

Again, I'll show you exactly where to find the current ratio. But for now, just keep in mind that, as value investors, we only invest in companies that have a current ratio of 1.5 or more.

Got it?

Good!

Moving right along. Let's discuss Criteria # 11: Quick Ratio.

11. QUICK RATIO

Before investing in a company's stock, make sure it has a Quick Ratio of 1.5 or above.

If criteria # 3 (ROIC) and criteria # 4 (ROE) were siblings, then criteria # 10 (Current Ratio) and criteria # 11 (Quick Ratio) are identical twins. It's unbelievable how similar these two ratios are. Truly, it is.

So, I will do my best to differentiate them for you. (Hopefully I do a good enough job).

Let's start out by simply defining quick ratio. The quick ratio is also a liquidity metric that measures how well a company can meet its short-term financial obligations. But the quick ratio differs from the current ratio in that the quick ratio takes into account more liquid assets (like cash and cash equivalents), and excludes less liquid assets (like inventory and property), in its calculation.

The current ratio formula takes into account assets that can take up to a year to sell, in order to be converted to cash (like inventory, or large real estate holdings). Whereas the quick ratio formula considers only assets that can be converted to cash in a few days, or even a few hours or minutes (like cash itself, or stocks and bonds).

Think of the "quick" part in quick ratio as meaning assets that can be liquidated the *fastest*, in order to pay for present liabilities.

Therefore, because current ratio assets are harder (or take longer) to liquidate than quick ratio assets, if you really want to measure a company's *true* liquidity power, the quick ratio is probably the more conservative formula to use.

The quick ratio formula is: Current Assets (*excluding* Inventories) / Current Liabilities.

I like to use both current and quick ratios, if only to have a better idea of how liquid a company is. But either ratio will suffice, though. As long as the company's quick—or current—ratio is 1.5 or above, you're good.

So, to close this section up, remember: Only invest in companies that have a quick ratio of 1.5 or above, because that suggests that the company has at least 50% more cash on hand than they do short-term debt. Which is never a bad thing.

Understood?

Cool.

Now, for our last criteria, Criteria # 12: Trend Numbers.

12. TREND NUMBERS

Before investing in a company's stock, make sure it has a steady and/or growing trend of Revenue, Earnings Per Share (or EPS), Book Value Per Share (or BVPS), Free Cash Flow (or FCF), and Working Capital, dating back ten years.

I call these five financial testers my "trend numbers." I'll keep this short and sweet. If the following five categories show steady declines in the past ten years, I would strongly suggest you pass on that particular investment—**even if the stock is selling at a discount to true value**. Why? Well, because it means that for some reason or another (usually, increased competition, or mismanagement) the company is losing its muster.

The five "trend numbers" categories you should track are:

1. **<u>Revenue</u>**: This is defined as how much of a company's products/services are sold during a fiscal period. As a value investor, you want to make sure that the company's overall revenue numbers are growing—or, at the very least, steady. Do not invest in a company whose sales numbers are plummeting, or unstable.

2. **Earnings Per Share (or EPS)**: This is defined as the portion of the company's profits which are allocated to each share of common stock. EPS shows how profitable a company is on a per share basis. As a value investor, you want to make sure that the company's EPS numbers are growing—or, at the very least, steady. Do not invest in a company whose EPS numbers are sinking, or volatile.
3. **Book Value Per Share (or BVPS)**: This is defined as the amount of money, per share, that a shareholder would get if the company were to dissolve. BVPS is basically the tangible net worth of the company. As a value investor, you want to make sure that the company's BVPS numbers are growing—or, at the very least, steady. Do not invest in a company whose BVPS numbers are falling, or unpredictable.
4. **Free Cash Flow (or FCF)**: This is defined as the amount of cash remaining after a company has paid off all of its capital expenditures. FCF is basically a financial metric that measures how much cash reserves a company generates per fiscal cycle. This is a very important number because if a company has lots of free cash flow, management can use that "extra" money to increase shareholder value by, for example, developing new products, making new acquisitions, eliminating debt, paying dividends, etc. As a value investor, you want to make sure that the company's FCF numbers are growing—or, at the very least, steady. Do not invest in a company whose FCF numbers are decreasing, or unsteady.
5. **Working Capital**: This is defined as the amount of cash a company has on hand to cover its day to day operations. Working capital is a very important number because if a company does not have enough cash on hand to meet its daily obligations, the company may be forced to borrow money (and thus incur debt), or, worse, file for bankruptcy (if they can't borrow anymore). As a value investor, you want to make sure that the company's working capital numbers are growing—or, at the very least, balanced. Do not invest in a company whose working capital numbers are tumbling, or fickle.

I include these trend numbers in the 12 criteria because they are supreme indicators of how healthy a company is. These five trend numbers are somewhat like the five vital organs in our bodies (brain, heart, kidney, liver, and lungs).

Most people are born healthy. But over the years, bad habits (smoking excessively, drinking excessively, poor nutrition, sedentariness, etc.) can cause even the fittest of bodies and organs to deteriorate.

The same applies for businesses.

At the start, businesses can oftentimes achieve miraculous growth and profitability (usually because they introduce a new product or service into the market). But as time goes by, competition, mismanagement, and other factors, may chip away at a company's profitability, and thus deteriorate its health.

I've come to understand that the latter is what usually happens to about 9 out of 10 businesses. Thus, only 10% of businesses are able to reach the plateau of success—and actually stay there[22].

Those are the ten percent you want to invest in.

Using the 12th criteria—Trend Numbers—will force you to analyze a company's health rating, dating back 10 years. And the way to figure that out is simple: If—over the course of the past ten years—a company's five trend numbers are rising, or, at the very least, level, provided a majority of the other 11 criteria are met, it's a safe bet that the company is a good investment. But if, on the other hand, the company's five trend numbers—dating back ten years—are plummeting or extremely volatile, well… even if the other 11 criteria are met, I would pass on the investment. The company may be fundamentally healthy in other areas, but if its vital organs (Sales, Earnings Per Share, Book Value Per Share, Free Cash Flow, and Working Capital) are declining, the entire body will soon capitulate.

And then you're fucked.

[22] http://www.forbes.com/sites/neilpatel/2015/01/16/90-of-startups-will-fail-heres-what-you-need-to-know-about-the-10/#378c3c1455e1

CHAPTER RECAP

So there you have it. These are the 12 criteria that are most important to a value investor. If you follow these twelve guidelines when picking stocks, you will minimize your risks and maximize your profits.

Now, for a quick recap.

Only consider buying stocks that meet 9 (or more) out of the following 12 criteria (with criteria number 1 and 12 being the two, must-have criteria):

1. **True Value**: The stock you're interested in buying must be selling at a discount to its *true value*, regardless of market price.
2. **Dividend**: The stock you're interested in buying must pay a dividend of at least 2.5% or more.
3. **ROIC**: The stock you're interested in purchasing must have a Return on Invested Capital rate of 10% or more.
4. **ROE**: The stock you're interested in acquiring must have a Return on Equity rate of 10% or more.
5. **Net Profit Margin**: The stock you're interested in obtaining must have a Net Profit Margin of 10% or more.
6. **P/E Ratio**: The stock you're interested in securing must have a Price to Earnings Ratio of 15 or less.
7. **Price/Sales Ratio**: The stock you're interested in getting must have a Price to Sales Ratio of 0.6 - 1.5.
8. **Price/Book Ratio**: The stock you're interested in ordering must have a Price to Book Ratio of 0.6 - 1.5.
9. **Debt/Equity Ratio**: The stock you're interested in acquiring must have a Debt to Equity Ratio of .50 or less.

10. **Current Ratio**: The stock you're interested in buying must have a Current Ratio of 1.5 or more.
11. **Quick Ratio**: The stock you're interested in purchasing must have a Quick Ratio of 1.5 or more.
12. **Trend Numbers**: The stock you're interested in picking must have a long history of increasing (or steady) Sales, Earnings Per Share, Book Value Per Share, Free Cash Flow, and Working Capital.

The only time you should not buy a stock, even if it meets nine or more of the twelve criteria, is when it fails to meet criteria 1 and 12. So, no matter how many of the criteria the stock meets, if it is overpriced (criteria 1), or if its trend numbers are declining (criteria 12), you should probably pass on that investment.

Now, let me be very clear. Again. **It is going to be extremely hard—damn near impossible—to find a stock that passes our 12-criteria standard**. That's because, no matter what corporate America tries to tell you—with its glossy, appealing ads and commercials—9 out of 10 businesses out there suck.

At least for investment purposes.

Don't get me wrong. A lot of companies' products and/or services may be good from a consumer-experience standpoint. But from an accounting perspective, most businesses out there are not as profitable as they seem.

But of course, these companies won't tell you that (they'd be idiots if they did). So, it is up to you, as an investor, to look past the sleek advertisements that these companies generate, and focus instead on the cold, hard financial facts, which can only be found in a company's annual reports.

That is where the *truth* lies.

And before investing a single dime of your hard-earned money, you'd better make sure that that company is properly valued and sustainably profitable. And the best way to do that is to use our 12-criteria checklist.

Got it?

Cool.

Now that you know *what* classifications to look for in an investment, I am going to show you *where* to find them. I use two websites to glean *all* of the information I need to complete my 12-criteria checklist.

Let's check those websites out.

CHAPTER 7

THE RESOURCES!

Hello again, y'all.

In this chapter, I am going to show you where to find the 12 criteria. And believe me when I tell you: It ain't no great mystery.

I use two, free websites to get all of the information that I need:

1. Marketwatch.com
2. Morningstar.com

Yep.

That's it.

With the internet being as advanced as it is, all of the valuable, financial information you could ever want on a company is at your fingertips. For free!

Literally.

With a few keystrokes, and several clicks of your mouse, the world of high finance becomes your oyster, to glean and plunder as you see fit.

The good thing about investing in the stock market is that publicly-owned companies *must* publish their financial data. So, if you know where to look, you can find any category of information you want.

And we—as value investors—are interested in finding information relevant to our 12-criteria checklist.

So, with no further ado, I re-introduce to you The 12 Criteria… and *where* to find them…

1. TRUE VALUE

We want to make sure that the price of the stock we're interested in is discounted—meaning, that the stock is selling below its true value.

Because *that's* where the bargain is.

In chapter 5 we talked about the income statement and balance sheet, two financial documents that provide us with two numbers needed to properly value the stock of a company.

The balance sheet provides us with a number called *total equity*, which is basically what you get when you subtract a company's liabilities from its assets. The resulting number (the total equity) is essentially the company's entire net worth.

The income statement provides us with a number called *diluted shares outstanding*, which is basically the amount of stocks that a company has out on the market.

When you divide the total equity by the diluted shares outstanding (Total Equity / Diluted Shares Outstanding) you come up with a figure that represents exactly what each individual stock of a company is *truly* worth.

The website that I use to determine whether the market price of a stock is undervalued or overvalued is marketwatch.com. I use this website because it not only shows me what the current market price of a stock is, but it also provides me with every stock market companies' published income statement and balance sheet information.

So, let's do a trial run to see how this works out. Let's use marketwatch.com to find out whether Walmart Corporation stock (ticker symbol WMT) is currently overvalued or discounted.

STEP #1: Open the online browser on your computer, and type in *MARKETWATCH.COM/INVESTING* in the address bar.

STEP #2: Once the webpage appears, click on the site's search box (which is accessible when you click on the little magnifying glass icon on the right side of the screen).

STEP #3: A search box should appear, and in that search box, type Walmart's ticker symbol: *WMT.*

STEP #4: An "OVERVIEW" page will appear, with a few details on Walmart's stock, including its market price (which is $75.78 as of this writing). On this page, you'll see a section entitled "*Key Data,*" and under it you'll find other tidbits of information, such as the company's "*Open,*" "*Day's Range,*" "*52-Week Range,*" "*Market Cap,*" "*Shares Outstanding,*" "*Public Float,*" "*BETA,*" "*Rev. Per Employee,*" "*P/E Ratio,*" "*EPS,*" "*Yield,*" "*Dividend,*" "*Ex-Dividend Date,*" "*Short Interest,*" "*% of Float Shorted,*" and "*Average Volume,*" to name a few. Above all of this information, you should see the following web links: "OVERVIEW," "PROFILE," "NEWS," "CHARTS," "FINANCIALS," "HISTORICAL QUOTES," "ANALYST ESTIMATES," "OPTIONS," "SEC FILINGS," and "INSIDERS." In order to find the first number we'll need (the Total Equity number), click on the link labeled "FINANCIALS."

STEP #5: After clicking on the "FINANCIALS" link, a new screen will appear with a new set of links: "INCOME STATEMENT," "BALANCE SHEET," and "CASH FLOW STATEMENT." To get our Total Equity number, click on the "BALANCE SHEET" link.

STEP #6: After clicking on the "BALANCE SHEET" link, a new screen will appear. If you look at the information on the screen, you'll notice that the screen is broken up into 2 sections: "*Assets*" (located at the top of the page) and "*Liabilities and Shareholders' Equity*" (located somewhere in the middle of the page). Our Total Equity number is located under the "*Liabilities & Shareholders' Equity*" section, at the very bottom of the page. It's actually the next to last line on the balance sheet. We want the Total Equity number that's located under the most recent year. As I am writing this, the most recently documented year on this balance sheet is 2016. And the Total Equity number for 2016 is 80.54B (or 80.54 billion dollars). Write this number down somewhere (or, remember it if you can).

STEP #7: After retrieving the Total Equity number from the "BALANCE SHEET" link, go back to the top of the screen, and click on the "INCOME STATEMENT" link. A new screen will appear. On this screen is the second number we need, the Diluted Shares Outstanding number. This number is located beneath the "*Net Income*" section, at the very bottom of the page. It's actually the next to last line on the income statement (right above the line "*EBITDA*"). We want the Diluted Shares Outstanding number that's located under the most recent year. As I am writing this, the most recently documented year on this income statement is 2016. And the Diluted Shares Outstanding number for 2016 is 3.11B (or 3.11 billion shares). Write this number down somewhere (or, remember it if you can).

STEP #8: Now that you have the two numbers you need (Total Equity and Diluted Shares Outstanding), let's do some simple math to figure out what each stock of WMT is worth. To accomplish this, we simply divide Total Equity by Diluted Shares Outstanding. So, for the purposes of this WMT example, the math will look like this: $80.54 billion (Total Equity) / 3.11 billion (Diluted Shares Outstanding) = 25.89. Which means that as of this writing, Walmart shares have a market price of $75.78 each, but are truly worth $25.89 per share.

So, you may be asking yourself, *what now*?

Well, viewing the situation through our value investors' lenses, it's a clear-cut fact that WMT stock is not a good bet right at the moment. Why? Well, because after crunching the numbers, our analysis (which we did above) shows us that WMT stock is highly overpriced. It's selling for $75.78 per share, but is truly worth $25.89 per share. Which means that its market price is 3 times higher than its true value price.

And that means that, even if the other 11 criteria points are met, we will not invest in WMT stock right now, due to its overvaluation by the market. What we *will* do though—*if* the other criteria numbers show promise—is keep WMT on our target list, and revisit the stock from time to time. If, in the future, the market reprices WMT stock at a price that represents a discount to its *true value* appraisal (provided the other criteria numbers are copacetic), then, and only then, will we consider purchasing WMT stock.

That' why it's important to complete a full 12-criteria evaluation of each stock you're interested in buying. Reason being, sometimes a stock's market price may be overvalued; but that doesn't necessarily mean that the stock is not a good investment. If most of the other criteria are met, that just means that the stock is not a good investment *right now*. But let's say, months from now, the market crashes, and the stock's price tumbles and falls beneath its true value, at that point, the stock may be worth buying. Because now it's selling at a discount.

So, now that we've determined what Walmart's true value is, let's move on to Criteria #2: Dividend. Let's stay with Walmart Corp. and use its stock (ticker symbol WMT) to show you how to find a company's dividend number online.

2. DIVIDEND

We want to make sure that the stock in question pays a dividend of at least 2.5% or more.

As I mentioned in chapter 6, some companies—though not all companies—pay you back a percentage of the money you invested. Thus, you get paid income simply for owning the stock.

A few companies pay dividends on a monthly basis. But in general, most companies pay out their dividends on a quarterly, or bi-annual, basis.

Companies usually pay dividends because their operations are profitable and are yielding excess cash. Thus, to maintain their investors' happiness—and loyalty—they share these profits with their stockholders.

For more detailed information on the dividend, re-read the section on dividends, which can be found in *Chapter 6: The 12 Criteria*. For the purposes of this chapter, though, I will merely show you *where* to find the dividend number. We will again use Walmart Corporation (ticker symbol WMT) as an example.

Ready?

Vamanos!

STEP #1: Open the online browser on your computer, and type in *MARKETWATCH.COM/INVESTING* in the address bar.

STEP #2: Once the webpage appears, click on the site's search box (which is accessible when you click on the little magnifying glass icon on the right side of the screen).

STEP #3: A search box should appear, and in that search box, type Walmart ticker symbol: *WMT*.

STEP #4: An "OVERVIEW" page will appear, with a few details on Walmart's stock, including its market price. On this page, you'll see a section entitled "*Key Data,*" and under it you'll find other tidbits of information, such as the company's "*Open,*" "*Day's Range,*" "*52-Week Range,*" "*Market Cap,*" "*Shares*

Outstanding," "*Public Float,*" "*BETA,*" "*Rev. Per Employee,*" "*P/E Ratio,*" "*EPS,*" "*Yield,*" "*Dividend,*" "*Ex-Dividend Date,*" "*Short Interest,*" "*% of Float Shorted,*" and "*Average Volume,*" to name a few. Above all of this information, you should see the following web links: "OVERVIEW," "PROFILE," "NEWS," "CHARTS," "FINANCIALS," "HISTORICAL QUOTES," "ANALYST ESTIMATES," "OPTIONS," "SEC FILINGS," and "INSIDERS."

STEP #5: What we are looking for is the dividend *yield*. This number reflects the percentage amount the company is paying out in dividends. To find the dividend yield, simply scroll down the "OVERVIEW" page. Under the "*Key Data*" section you will find a percentage number under the category "*Yield.*" As of this writing, Walmart Corporation is paying a dividend yield of 2.69%.

So, you may be asking yourself, *what now*?

Well, we can see quite plainly, that WMT meets our second criteria. Our dividend criteria requires us to invest only in companies that have a dividend yield of 2.5% or more. Walmart has a dividend of 2.6%.

Hoorah!

So now that we've determined what Walmart's dividend is, let's move on to Criteria #3: ROIC (or, Return on Invested Capital). Let's stay with Walmart Corp. and use its stock (ticker symbol WMT) to show you how to locate a company's ROIC number online.

3. ROIC

We want to make sure that the stock in question has a Return on Invested Capital rate of at least 10% or more.

ROIC is used to assess how efficient a company is at investing (and multiplying) the money under its control.

Meaning, *your* hard-earned money.

So, it would behoove you to find a company that has a long-standing record of flipping their investors' dough as exponentially, and as carefully, as possible.

For more detailed information on the dividend, re-read the section on ROIC, which can be found in *Chapter 6: The 12 Criteria*. For the purposes of this chapter, though, I will merely show you *where* to find the ROIC number. We will again use Walmart Corporation (ticker symbol WMT) as an example.

STEP #1: Open the online browser on your computer, and type in *MARKETWATCH.COM/INVESTING* in the address bar.

STEP #2: Once the webpage appears, click on the site's search box (which is accessible when you click on the little magnifying glass icon on the right side of the screen).

STEP #3: A search box should appear, and in that search box, type Walmart ticker symbol: *WMT.*

STEP #4: An "OVERVIEW" page will appear, with a few details on Walmart's stock, including its market price. On this page, you'll see a section entitled "*Key Data,*" and under it you'll find other tidbits of information, such as the company's "*Open,*" "*Day's Range,*" "*52-Week Range,*" "*Market Cap,*" "*Shares Outstanding,*" "*Public Float,*" "*BETA,*" "*Rev. Per Employee,*" "*P/E Ratio,*" "*EPS,*" "*Yield,*" "*Dividend,*" "*Ex-Dividend Date,*" "*Short Interest,*" "*% of Float Shorted,*" and "*Average Volume,*" to name a few. Above all of this information, you should see the following web links: "OVERVIEW," "PROFILE," "NEWS," "CHARTS," "FINANCIALS," "HISTORICAL QUOTES," "ANALYST ESTIMATES," "OPTIONS," "SEC FILINGS," and "INSIDERS." In order to find the ROIC number, click on the link labeled "PROFILE."

STEP #5: A new page will appear. The page will be broken into several categories. The categories are "*Company Description,*" "*Valuation,*" "*Profitability,*" "*Efficiency,*" "*Capital Structure,*" "*Liquidity,*" "*Officers and Executives,*" "*Insider Actions,*" "*MarketWatch News on WMT,*" to name a few. The ROIC number can be found under the category "*Profitability.*" It is the eighth number from the top, the very last number under the "*Profitability*" category. As I am writing this, Walmart's ROIC number is 11.16. Which means 11.16%.

So, what now?

Well, we can see quite plainly, that WMT meets our third criteria. Our ROIC criteria requires us to invest only in companies that have a return on invested capital rate of at least 10% or more. Walmart has a ROIC of 11.16%.

Hell yeah!!

So now that we've determined what Walmart's ROIC is, let's move on to Criteria #4: ROE (or, Return on Equity). Let's stay with Walmart Corp. and use its stock (ticker symbol WMT) to show you how to locate a company's ROE number online.

4. ROE

We want to make sure that the stock in question has a Return on Equity rate of at least 10% or more.

ROE—like ROIC—is used to assess how efficient a company is at investing (and multiplying) the money under its control.

The difference between ROIC and ROE is that ROIC is used by analysts to compare the profitability of companies in *different* sectors (for example, a fast-food chain company, and a car manufacturing company). Whereas ROE is used to compare the profitability of companies that are within the *same* sector (for example a fast-food chain and another fast-food chain).

For more detailed information on ROE, re-read the section on ROE, which can be found in *Chapter 6: The 12 Criteria.* But for the purposes of this chapter, I will merely show you *where* to find the ROE number. We will again use Walmart Corporation (ticker symbol WMT) as an example.

STEP #1: Open the online browser on your computer, and type in *MARKETWATCH.COM/INVESTING* in the address bar.

STEP #2: Once the webpage appears, click on the site's search box (which is accessible when you click on the little magnifying glass icon on the right side of the screen).

STEP #3: A search box should appear, and in that search box, type Walmart ticker symbol: *WMT.*

STEP #4: An "OVERVIEW" page will appear, with a few details on Walmart's stock, including its market price. On this page, you'll see a section entitled "*Key Data,*" and under it you'll find other tidbits of information, such as the company's "*Open,*" "*Day's Range,*" "*52-Week Range,*" "*Market Cap,*" "*Shares Outstanding,*" "*Public Float,*" "*BETA,*" "*Rev. Per Employee,*" "*P/E Ratio,*" "*EPS,*" "*Yield,*" "*Dividend,*" "*Ex-Dividend Date,*" "*Short Interest,*" "*% of Float Shorted,*" and "*Average Volume,*" to name a few. Above all of this information, you should see the following web links: "OVERVIEW," "PROFILE," "NEWS," "CHARTS," "FINANCIALS," "HISTORICAL QUOTES," "ANALYST ESTIMATES," "OPTIONS," "SEC FILINGS," and "INSIDERS." In order to find the ROIC number, click on the link labeled "PROFILE."

STEP #5: A new page will appear. The page will be broken into several categories. The categories are "*Company Description*," "*Valuation*," "*Profitability*," "*Efficiency*," "*Capital Structure*," "*Liquidity*," "*Officers and Executives*," "*Insider Actions*," "*MarketWatch News on WMT*," to name a few. The ROE number can be found under the category "*Profitability*." It is the sixth number from the top under the "*Profitability*" category. As I am writing this, Walmart's ROE number is 17.23. Which means 17.23%.

So, what now?

Well, we can see quite plainly, that WMT meets our fourth criteria. Our ROE criteria requires us to invest only in companies that have a return on equity rate of at least 10% or more. Walmart has a ROE of 17.23%.

Fuck yeah!!

So now that we've determined what Walmart's ROE is, let's move on to Criteria #5: Net Profit Margin. Let's stay with Walmart Corp. and use its stock (ticker symbol WMT) to show you how to locate a company's Net Profit Margin number online.

5. NET PROFIT MARGIN

We want to make sure that the stock in question has a Net Profit Margin rate of at least 10% or more.

The net profit margin is the percentage of total revenue that's left after the company has finished paying off all of their bills and expenses.

For more detailed information on the net profit margin, re-read the section on it, which can be found in *Chapter 6: The 12 Criteria*. But for the purposes of this chapter, I will merely show you *where* to find the Net Profit Margin number. We will again use Walmart Corporation (ticker symbol WMT) as an example.

STEP #1: Open the online browser on your computer, and type in *MARKETWATCH.COM/INVESTING* in the address bar.

STEP #2: Once the webpage appears, click on the site's search box (which is accessible when you click on the little magnifying glass icon on the right side of the screen).

STEP #3: A search box should appear, and in that search box, type Walmart ticker symbol: *WMT*.

STEP #4: An "OVERVIEW" page will appear, with a few details on Walmart's stock, including its market price. On this page, you'll see a section entitled "*Key Data,*" and under it you'll find other tidbits of information, such as the company's "*Open,*" "*Day's Range,*" "*52-Week Range,*" "*Market Cap,*" "*Shares Outstanding,*" "*Public Float,*" "*BETA,*" "*Rev. Per Employee,*" "*P/E Ratio,*" "*EPS,*" "*Yield,*" "*Dividend,*" "*Ex-Dividend Date,*" "*Short Interest,*" "*% of Float Shorted,*" and "*Average Volume,*" to name a few. Above all of this information, you should see the following web links: "OVERVIEW," "PROFILE," "NEWS," "CHARTS," "FINANCIALS," "HISTORICAL QUOTES," "ANALYST ESTIMATES," "OPTIONS," "SEC FILINGS," and "INSIDERS." In order to find the Net Profit Margin number, click on the link labeled "PROFILE."

STEP #5: A new page will appear. The page will be broken into several categories. The categories are "*Company Description,*" "*Valuation,*" "*Profitability,*" "*Efficiency,*" "*Capital Structure,*" "*Liquidity,*" "*Officers and Executives,*" "*Insider Actions,*" "*MarketWatch News on WMT,*" to name a few. The Net Profit Margin number can be found under the category "*Profitability.*" It is the fourth number from the top, under the "*Profitability*" category. It reads "Net Margin." As I am writing this, Walmart's Net Margin number is 2.81. Which means 2.81%.

So, what now?

Well, we can see quite plainly, that WMT does not meet our fifth criteria. Our Net Profit Margin criteria requires us to invest only in companies that have a net margin rate of at least 10% or more. Walmart has a Net margin of 2.81%.

Bummer!

So now that we've determined what Walmart's Net Profit Margin is, let's move on to Criteria #6: P/E Ratio (or Price-to-Earnings Ratio). Let's stay with Walmart Corp. and use its stock (ticker symbol WMT) to show you how to locate a company's P/E Ratio number online.

6. P/E RATIO

We want to make sure that the stock in question has a P/E Ratio of 15 or less.

The P/E Ratio represents a stock's market price (on a per-share basis), relative to the stock's total earnings (also on a per-share basis). So if a company has a PE ratio of 10, that means that the company's market price is valued at ten times what the company is earning.

For value investors, the lower the PE ratio, the better. Why? Well, because if the PE ratio is too high, it means that the stock is overpriced. That is why we only select stocks with PE ratios of 15 or less.

For more detailed information on the PE ratio, re-read the section on it, which can be found in *Chapter 6: The 12 Criteria*. But for the purposes of this chapter, I will merely show you *where* to find the PE ratio number. We will again use Walmart Corporation (ticker symbol WMT) as an example.

STEP #1: Open the online browser on your computer, and type in *MARKETWATCH.COM/INVESTING* in the address bar.

STEP #2: Once the webpage appears, click on the site's search box (which is accessible when you click on the little magnifying glass icon on the right side of the screen).

STEP #3: A search box should appear, and in that search box, type Walmart ticker symbol: *WMT*.

STEP #4: An "OVERVIEW" page will appear, with a few details on Walmart's stock, including its market price. On this page, you'll see a section entitled "*Key Data,*" and under it you'll find other tidbits of information, such as the company's "*Open,*" "*Day's Range,*" "*52-Week Range,*" "*Market Cap,*" "*Shares Outstanding,*" "*Public Float,*" "*BETA,*" "*Rev. Per Employee,*" "*P/E Ratio,*" "*EPS,*" "*Yield,*" "*Dividend,*" "*Ex-Dividend Date,*" "*Short Interest,*" "*% of Float Shorted,*" and "*Average Volume,*" to name a few. Above all of this information, you should see the following web links: "OVERVIEW," "PROFILE," "NEWS," "CHARTS," "FINANCIALS," "HISTORICAL QUOTES," "ANALYST ESTIMATES," "OPTIONS," "SEC

FILINGS," and "INSIDERS." In order to find the PE Ratio number, click on the link labeled "PROFILE."

STEP #5: A new page will appear. The page will be broken into several categories. The categories are "*Company Description*," "*Valuation*," "*Profitability*," "*Efficiency*," "*Capital Structure*," "*Liquidity*," "*Officers and Executives*," "*Insider Actions*," "*MarketWatch News on WMT*," to name a few. The PE Ratio number can be found under the category "*Valuation*." It is the first number from the top, under the "*Valuation*" category. It reads "P/E Current." As I am writing this, Walmart's P/E Ratio number is 17.18.

So, what now?

Well, we can see quite plainly, that WMT does not meet our sixth criteria. Our PE Ratio criteria requires us to invest only in companies that have a PE ratio of 15 or less. Walmart has a PE ratio of 17.81. Which means that it is overpriced.

Sucks!

So now that we've determined what Walmart's PE ratio is, let's move on to Criteria #7: Price/Sales Ratio. Let's stay with Walmart Corp. and use its stock (ticker symbol WMT) to show you how to locate a company's P/S Ratio number online.

7. PS RATIO

Before investing in a company's stock, we want to make sure it has a Price to Sales Ratio (or PS ratio) between 0.6 and 1.5.

The PS ratio—like the PE ratio—is a valuation metric. It is merely the market price of a company's stock, relative to the annual sales generated by the company. So if a company has a PS ratio of 5, that means that the company's market price is valued at 5 times what the company generated in sales in the last fiscal year.

As value investors, we want to invest in companies with PS ratios between 0.6 – 1.5

For more detailed information on the PS ratio, re-read the section on it, which can be found in *Chapter 6: The 12 Criteria.* But for the purposes of this chapter, I will merely show you *where* to find the PS ratio number. We will again use Walmart Corporation (ticker symbol WMT) as an example.

STEP #1: Open the online browser on your computer, and type in *MARKETWATCH.COM/INVESTING* in the address bar.

STEP #2: Once the webpage appears, click on the site's search box (which is accessible when you click on the little magnifying glass icon on the right side of the screen).

STEP #3: A search box should appear, and in that search box, type Walmart ticker symbol: *WMT.*

STEP #4: An "OVERVIEW" page will appear, with a few details on Walmart's stock, including its market price. On this page, you'll see a section entitled "*Key Data,*" and under it you'll find other tidbits of information, such as the company's "*Open,*" "*Day's Range,*" "*52-Week Range,*" "*Market Cap,*" "*Shares Outstanding,*" "*Public Float,*" "*BETA,*" "*Rev. Per Employee,*" "*P/E Ratio,*" "*EPS,*" "*Yield,*" "*Dividend,*" "*Ex-Dividend Date,*" "*Short Interest,*" "*% of Float Shorted,*" and "*Average Volume,*" to name a few. Above all of this information, you should see the following web links: "OVERVIEW," "PROFILE," "NEWS," "CHARTS," "FINANCIALS," "HISTORICAL QUOTES," "ANALYST ESTIMATES," "OPTIONS," "SEC FILINGS," and "INSIDERS." In order to find the PE Ratio number, click on the link labeled "PROFILE."

STEP #5: A new page will appear. The page will be broken into several categories. The categories are "*Company Description,*" "*Valuation,*" "*Profitability,*" "*Efficiency,*" "*Capital Structure,*" "*Liquidity,*" "*Officers and Executives,*" "*Insider Actions,*" "*MarketWatch News on WMT,*" to name a few. The PS Ratio number can be found under the category "*Valuation.*" It is the fourth number from the top, under the "*Valuation*" category. It reads "Price to Sales Ratio." As I am writing this, Walmart's PS Ratio number is 0.43.

So, what now?

Well, as we can see, WMT does not meet our seventh criteria. Our PS Ratio criteria requires us to invest only in companies with PS ratios between 0.6 – 1.5. Walmart has a PS ratio of 0.48. Which is not enough.

Oh well…

So now that we've determined what Walmart's PS ratio is, let's move on to Criteria #8: Price/Book Ratio (or PB Ratio). Let's stay with Walmart Corp. and use its stock (ticker symbol WMT) to show you how to locate a company's PB Ratio number online.

8. PB RATIO

Before investing in a company's stock, we want to make sure it has a Price to Book Ratio (or PB ratio) between 0.6 - 1.5.

The PB ratio (again, like the PE and PS ratios) is a valuation metric. It represents the company's market price, relative to its tangible net worth (or true value). So if a company has a PB ratio of 10, that means that the company's market price is valued at 10 times what the company is actually worth.

Would you buy something—I don't care what the fuck it is—that was selling for 10 times its real worth? (I'd like to think not).

Well neither would a value investor. That is why a value investor only invests in companies with PB ratios between 0.6 – 1.5.

For more detailed information on the PB ratio, re-read the section on it, which can be found in *Chapter 6: The 12 Criteria.* But for the purposes of this chapter, I will merely show you *where* to find the PB ratio number. We will again use Walmart Corporation (ticker symbol WMT) as an example.

STEP #1: Open the online browser on your computer, and type in *MARKETWATCH.COM/INVESTING* in the address bar.

STEP #2: Once the webpage appears, click on the site's search box (which is accessible when you click on the little magnifying glass icon on the right side of the screen).

STEP #3: A search box should appear, and in that search box, type Walmart ticker symbol: *WMT.*

STEP #4: An "OVERVIEW" page will appear, with a few details on Walmart's stock, including its market price. On this page, you'll see a section entitled "*Key Data,*" and under it you'll find other tidbits of information, such as the company's

"*Open,*" "*Day's Range,*" "*52-Week Range,*" "*Market Cap,*" "*Shares Outstanding,*" "*Public Float,*" "*BETA,*" "*Rev. Per Employee,*" "*P/E Ratio,*" "*EPS,*" "*Yield,*" "*Dividend,*" "*Ex-Dividend Date,*" "*Short Interest,*" "*% of Float Shorted,*" and "*Average Volume,*" to name a few. Above all of this information, you should see the following web links: "OVERVIEW," "PROFILE," "NEWS," "CHARTS," "FINANCIALS," "HISTORICAL QUOTES," "ANALYST ESTIMATES," "OPTIONS," "SEC FILINGS," and "INSIDERS." In order to find the PE Ratio number, click on the link labeled "PROFILE."

STEP #5: A new page will appear. The page will be broken into several categories. The categories are "*Company Description,*" "*Valuation,*" "*Profitability,*" "*Efficiency,*" "*Capital Structure,*" "*Liquidity,*" "*Officers and Executives,*" "*Insider Actions,*" "*MarketWatch News on WMT,*" to name a few. The PB Ratio number can be found under the category "*Valuation.*" It is the fifth number from the top, under the "*Valuation*" category. It reads "Price to Book Ratio." As I am writing this, Walmart's PB Ratio number is 2.61.

So, what now?

Well, we can see quite plainly, that WMT does not meet our eighth criteria. Our PB Ratio criteria requires us to invest only in companies with PB ratios between 0.6 – 1.5. Walmart has a PB ratio of 2.61. Which is way too much.

Well, can't win 'em all….

So now that we've determined what Walmart's PB ratio is, let's move on to Criteria #9: Debt/Equity Ratio (or DE Ratio). Let's stay with Walmart Corp. and use its stock (ticker symbol WMT) to show you how to locate a company's DE Ratio number online.

9. DE RATIO

Before investing in a company's stock, make sure it has a Debt to Equity Ratio (or DE ratio) below .50 (or 50%).

The DE ratio is also a valuation metric (like the PE, PS, and PB ratios). The DE ratio represents the company's total debt, relative to its equity (that is to say, all of the company's assets, after all liabilities have been accounted for).

When a company has a DE ratio of over .50, it means that the company has more debt than assets. Which leads us to infer that the company is not being managed very well.

We want no parts of such a company. That is why, as value investors, we require a DE ratio below .50.

For more detailed information on the DE ratio, re-read the section on it, which can be found in *Chapter 6: The 12 Criteria*. But for the purposes of this chapter, I will merely show you *where* to find the DE ratio number. We will again use Walmart Corporation (ticker symbol WMT) as an example.

STEP #1: Open the online browser on your computer, and type in *MARKETWATCH.COM/INVESTING* in the address bar.

STEP #2: Once the webpage appears, click on the site's search box (which is accessible when you click on the little magnifying glass icon on the right side of the screen).

STEP #3: A search box should appear, and in that search box, type Walmart ticker symbol: *WMT*.

STEP #4: An "OVERVIEW" page will appear, with a few details on Walmart's stock, including its market price. On this page, you'll see a section entitled "*Key Data*," and under it you'll find other tidbits of information, such as the company's "*Open*," "*Day's Range*," "*52-Week Range*," "*Market Cap*," "*Shares Outstanding*," "*Public Float*," "*BETA*," "*Rev. Per Employee*," "*P/E Ratio*," "*EPS*," "*Yield*," "*Dividend*," "*Ex-Dividend Date*," "*Short Interest*," "*% of Float Shorted*," and "*Average Volume*," to name a few. Above all of this information, you should see the following web links: "OVERVIEW," "PROFILE," "NEWS," "CHARTS," "FINANCIALS," "HISTORICAL QUOTES," "ANALYST ESTIMATES," "OPTIONS," "SEC FILINGS," and "INSIDERS." In order to find the DE Ratio number, click on the link labeled "PROFILE."

STEP #5: A new page will appear. The page will be broken into several categories. The categories are "*Company Description*," "*Valuation*," "*Profitability*," "*Efficiency*," "*Capital Structure*," "*Liquidity*," "*Officers and Executives*," "*Insider Actions*," "*MarketWatch News on WMT*," to name a few. The DE Ratio number can be found under the category "*Valuation*." It is the last number from the top, under the "*Valuation*" category. It reads "Total Debt to Enterprise Value." As I am writing this, Walmart's Total Debt to Enterprise Value is .18.

So, what now?

Well, we can see quite plainly, that WMT meets our ninth criteria. Our DE Ratio criteria requires us to invest only in companies that have a DE ratio of .50 or less. Walmart has a DE ratio of .18.

Great!

So now that we've determined what Walmart's DE Ratio is, let's move on to Criteria #10: Current Ratio. Let's stay with Walmart Corp. and use its stock (ticker symbol WMT) to show you how to locate a company's Current Ratio number online.

10. CURRENT RATIO

Before investing in a company's stock, make sure it has a Current Ratio of 1.5 or more.

The current ratio is not a valuation metric, but rather a liquidity metric. It measures a company's ability to pay its short-term liabilities (or debts) with its current assets.

For more detailed information on the Current ratio, re-read the section on it, which can be found in *Chapter 6: The 12 Criteria*. But for the purposes of this chapter, I will merely show you *where* to find the Current ratio number. We will again use Walmart Corporation (ticker symbol WMT) as an example.

<u>STEP #1</u>: Open the online browser on your computer, and type in *MARKETWATCH.COM/INVESTING* in the address bar.

<u>STEP #2</u>: Once the webpage appears, click on the site's search box (which is accessible when you click on the little magnifying glass icon on the right side of the screen).

<u>STEP #3</u>: A search box should appear, and in that search box, type Walmart ticker symbol: *WMT*.

<u>STEP #4</u>: An "OVERVIEW" page will appear, with a few details on Walmart's stock, including its market price. On this page, you'll see a section entitled "*Key Data,*" and under it you'll find other tidbits of information, such as the company's "*Open,*" "*Day's Range,*" "*52-Week Range,*" "*Market Cap,*" "*Shares Outstanding,*" "*Public Float,*" "*BETA,*" "*Rev. Per Employee,*" "*P/E Ratio,*" "*EPS,*" "*Yield,*" "*Dividend,*" "*Ex-Dividend Date,*" "*Short Interest,*" "*% of Float Shorted,*" and "*Average Volume,*" to name a few. Above all of this information, you should

see the following web links: "OVERVIEW," "PROFILE," "NEWS," "CHARTS," "FINANCIALS," "HISTORICAL QUOTES," "ANALYST ESTIMATES," "OPTIONS," "SEC FILINGS," and "INSIDERS." In order to find the Current Ratio number, click on the link labeled "PROFILE."

STEP #5: A new page will appear. The page will be broken into several categories. The categories are "*Company Description*," "*Valuation*," "*Profitability*," "*Efficiency*," "*Capital Structure*," "*Liquidity*," "*Officers and Executives*," "*Insider Actions*," "*MarketWatch News on WMT*," to name a few. The Current Ratio number can be found under the category "*Liquidity*." It is the first number under the "*Liquidity*" category. It reads "Current Ratio." As I am writing this, Walmart's Current Ratio is .86.

So, what do we do now?

Well, we can see quite plainly, that WMT does not meet our tenth criteria. Our Current Ratio criteria requires us to invest only in companies that have a Current Ratio of 1.5 or more. Walmart has a current ratio of only .86, which is not enough.

Sorry, Wally...

So now that we've determined what Walmart's Current Ratio is, let's move on to Criteria #11: Quick Ratio. Let's stay with Walmart Corp. and use its stock (ticker symbol WMT) to show you how to locate a company's Quick Ratio number online.

11. QUICK RATIO

Before investing in a company's stock, make sure it has a Quick Ratio of 1.5 or more.

The quick ratio is also a liquidity metric, just like the current ratio. In fact, both are identical, except for one minor difference. The current ratio formula takes into account assets that can take up to a year to sell, in order to be converted to cash (like inventory, or large real estate holdings). Whereas the quick ratio formula considers only assets that can be converted to cash in a few days, or even a few hours or minutes (like cash itself, or stocks and bonds).

For more detailed information on the quick ratio, re-read the section on it, which can be found in *Chapter 6: The 12 Criteria.* But for the purposes of this chapter, I will merely show you *where* to find the quick ratio number. We will again use Walmart Corporation (ticker symbol WMT) as an example.

STEP #1: Open the online browser on your computer, and type in *MARKETWATCH.COM/INVESTING* in the address bar.

STEP #2: Once the webpage appears, click on the site's search box (which is accessible when you click on the little magnifying glass icon on the right side of the screen).

STEP #3: A search box should appear, and in that search box, type Walmart ticker symbol: *WMT.*

STEP #4: An "OVERVIEW" page will appear, with a few details on Walmart's stock, including its market price. On this page, you'll see a section entitled "*Key Data,*" and under it you'll find other tidbits of information, such as the company's "*Open,*" "*Day's Range,*" "*52-Week Range,*" "*Market Cap,*" "*Shares Outstanding,*" "*Public Float,*" "*BETA,*" "*Rev. Per Employee,*" "*P/E Ratio,*" "*EPS,*" "*Yield,*" "*Dividend,*" "*Ex-Dividend Date,*" "*Short Interest,*" "*% of Float Shorted,*" and "*Average Volume,*" to name a few. Above all of this information, you should see the following web links: "OVERVIEW," "PROFILE," "NEWS," "CHARTS," "FINANCIALS," "HISTORICAL QUOTES," "ANALYST ESTIMATES," "OPTIONS," "SEC FILINGS," and "INSIDERS." In order to find the Quick Ratio number, click on the link labeled "PROFILE."

STEP #5: A new page will appear. The page will be broken into several categories. The categories are "*Company Description,*" "*Valuation,*" "*Profitability,*" "*Efficiency,*" "*Capital Structure,*" "*Liquidity,*" "*Officers and Executives,*" "*Insider Actions,*" "*MarketWatch News on WMT,*" to name a few. The Quick Ratio number can be found under the category "*Liquidity.*" It is the second number under the "*Liquidity*" category. It reads "Quick Ratio." As I am writing this, Walmart's Quick Ratio is .22.

So, what do we do now?

Well, we can see quite plainly, that WMT does not meet our tenth criteria. Our Quick Ratio criteria requires us to invest only in companies that have a Current Ratio of 1.5 or more. Walmart has a quick ratio of only .22, which is not enough.

Wally comes up short, yet again.

So now that we've determined what Walmart's Quick Ratio is, let's move on to the last criteria, Criteria #12: Trend Numbers. Let's stay with Walmart Corp. and use its stock (ticker symbol WMT) to show you how to locate a company's Quick Ratio number online.

12. TREND NUMBER

Before investing in a company's stock, make sure it has a steady and/or growing trend of Revenue, Earnings Per Share (or EPS), Book Value Per Share (or BVPS), Free Cash Flow (or FCF), and Working Capital, dating back ten years.

For more detailed information on the Trend Numbers, re-read the section on it, which can be found in *Chapter 6: The 12 Criteria.* But for the purposes of this chapter, I will merely show you *where* to find the trend numbers.

Unlike like the other 11 criteria numbers, we will be using the Morningstar.com website to find the Trend Numbers (instead of Marketwatch.com). We will again use Walmart Corporation (ticker symbol WMT) as an example.

STEP #1: Open the online browser on your computer, and type in *MORNINGSTAR.COM* in the address bar.

STEP #2: Once the webpage appears, point your curser on, and click, inside the site's search box (which can be found at the very top of the page).

STEP #3: Type Walmart's ticker symbol in the search box: *WMT*, and click enter.

STEP #4: "A new page will appear, with a few details on Walmart's stock, including its market price. On this page, you'll also see the following web links at the top of the screen: "QUOTE," "CHART," "STOCK ANALYSIS," "PERFORMANCE," "KEY RATIOS," "FINANCIALS," "VALUATION," "INSIDERS," "OWNERSHIP," "FILINGS," and "BONDS." Click on the "KEY RATIOS" link.

STEP #5: A new screen will appear. The screen will be broken into two major categories: "*Financials*" and "*Key Ratios*." All of the five trend numbers can be found under the "*Financials*" category.

1. **Revenue**: This is defined as how much of a company's products/services are sold during a fiscal period. As a value investor, you want to make sure that the company's overall revenue numbers are growing—or, at the very least, steady. Do not invest in a company whose revenue numbers are plummeting, or unstable. The revenue number is the first trend number under the "Financials" section. It will be broken down into years. Follow the years across the page, from left to right. Make sure that the company's revenue is increasing (or at the very least, remaining steady) with each passing year. At the moment of this writing, dating back to 2008, until now, WMT's revenues increased every year, until 2016, when it took a slight dip from the previous year. But one bad year out of ten is not cause for too much concern. WMT's revenue stream has proven to be strong for the past ten years.
2. **Earnings Per Share (or EPS)**: This is defined as the portion of the company's profits which are allocated to each share of common stock. Earnings Per Share shows how profitable a company is on a per share basis. As a value investor, you want to make sure that the company's EPS numbers are growing—or, at the very least, steady. Do not invest in a company whose Earnings Per Share numbers are sinking, or volatile. The Earnings Per Share number is the sixth number from the top. It will be broken down into years. Follow the years across the page, from left to right. Make sure that the company's earnings per share are increasing (or at the very least, remaining steady) with each passing year. At the moment of this writing, dating back to 2008, until now, WMT's Earnings Per Share increased every year, until 2014, when it took a slight dip from the previous year, and continued to tumble and/or experience volatility for the remaining years leading up to the present. WMT's volatile Earnings Per Share pattern is a cause for concern.
3. **Book Value Per Share (or BVPS)**: This is defined as the amount of money, per share, that a shareholder would get if the company were to dissolve. BVPS is basically the tangible net worth of the company. As a value investor, you want to make sure that the company's BVPS numbers are growing—or, at the very least, steady. Do not invest in a company whose BVPS numbers are falling, or unpredictable. The Book

Value Per Share number is the tenth number from the top. It will be broken down into years. Follow the years across the page, from left to right. Make sure that the company's BVPS is increasing (or at the very least, remaining steady) with each passing year. At the moment of this writing, dating back to 2008, until now, WMT's Book Value per Share has increased every year, without dipping once. WMT's Book Value Per Share pattern has proven to be strong for the past ten years.

4. **Free Cash Flow (or FCF)**: This is defined as the amount of cash remaining after a company has paid off all of its capital expenditures. FCF is basically a financial metric that measures how much cash reserves a company generates per fiscal cycle. This is a very important number because if a company has lots of free cash flow, management can use that "extra" money to increase shareholder value by, for example, developing new products, making new acquisitions, eliminating debt, paying dividends, etc. As a value investor, you want to make sure that the company's FCF numbers are growing—or, at the very least, steady. Do not invest in a company whose FCF numbers are decreasing, or unsteady. The Free Cash Flow number is the thirteenth number from the top. It will be broken down into years. Follow the years across the page, from left to right. Make sure that the company's FCF is increasing (or at the very least, remaining steady) with each passing year. At the moment of this writing, dating back to 2008, until now, WMT's Free Cash Flow has increased every year until 2011, when it took a slight dip from the previous year, and continued to tumble and/or experience volatility for the remaining years leading up to the present. Despite the fact that WMT's Free Cash Flow numbers are in the positive, the volatility of said numbers is a slight cause for concern.

5. **Working Capital**: This is defined as the amount of cash a company has on hand to cover its day to day operations. Working capital is a very important number because if a company does not have enough cash on hand to meet its daily obligations, the company may be forced to borrow money (and thus incur debt), or, worse, file for bankruptcy (if they can't borrow anymore). As a value investor, you want to make sure that the company's working capital numbers are growing—or, at the very least, balanced. Do not invest in a company

whose working capital numbers are tumbling, or fickle. The Working Capital number is the fifteenth (and very last) number from the top. It will be broken down into years. Follow the years across the page, from left to right. Make sure that the company's Working Capital is increasing (or at the very least, remaining steady) with each passing year. At the moment of this writing, dating back to 2008, until now, WMT's Working Capital has been in the negative. Right away, this should be a cause for heavy concern.

Chapter Recap

So, my dear reader. Now that we've taken a glance at all of Walmart's 12 criteria standards, what's the next step?

Well, it's simple, actually.

We tally up how much of our 12 criteria Walmart (or whatever company you're interested in investing in) actually met. So let's go down the checklist for the Walmart analysis we completed in this chapter:

1. True Value:
   a. Question: Is Walmart's stock selling at a discount to its true value?
   b. Answer: No.
   c. Grade: Fail.

2. Dividend:
   a. Question: Does Walmart's stock currently pay a dividend of 2.5% or more?
   b. Answer: Yes.
   c. Grade: Pass.

3. Return on Invested Capital (ROIC):
   a. Question: Does Walmart's stock currently have an ROIC of 10% or more?
   b. Answer: Yes.
   c. Grade: Pass.

4. Return on Equity (ROE):
   a. Question: Does Walmart's stock currently have an ROE of 10% or more?

   b. Answer: Yes.
   c. Grade: Pass.

5. Net Profit Margin:
   a. Question: Does Walmart's stock currently have a Net Profit Margin rate of 10% or more?
   b. Answer: No.
   c. Grade: Fail.

6. Price-to-Earning Ratio (or PE Ratio):
   a. Question: Does Walmart's stock currently have a PE Ratio of 15 or less?
   b. Answer: No.
   c. Grade: Fail.

7. Price-to-Sales Ratio (or PS Ratio):
   a. Question: Does Walmart's stock currently have a PS Ratio of 0.6-1.5?
   b. Answer: No.
   c. Grade: Fail.

8. Price-to-Book Ratio (or PB Ratio):
   a. Question: Does Walmart's stock currently have a PB Ratio of 0.6-1.5?
   b. Answer: No.
   c. Grade: Fail.

9. Debt-to-Equity Ratio (or DE Ratio):
   a. Question: Does Walmart's stock currently have a DE Ratio below .50?
   b. Answer: Yes.
   c. Grade: Pass.

10. Current Ratio:
   a. Question: Does Walmart's stock currently have a Current Ratio or 1.5 or more?

b. **Answer**: No.
c. **Grade**: Fail.

11. **Quick Ratio**:
    a. **Question**: Does Walmart's stock currently have a Quick Ratio or 1.5 or more?
    b. **Answer**: No.
    c. **Grade**: Fail.

12. **Trend Numbers**:
    a. **Question**: Have all five of Walmart's Trend Numbers shown steady increase, or stability, in the past ten years?
    b. **Answer**: No.
    c. **Grade**: Fail.

So, does Walmart get a passing grade?

Well let's see. Walmart met 4 out of the 12 criteria. So, Walmart's final grade is (drum roll please….) 33% (4/12 = .33).

Which fucking blows!

Because for a stock to pass our muster, it must meet, at the very least, 9 out of the 12 criteria (which is a 75% rating). And it must **always** satisfy the first and last criteria (*True Value* and *Trend Numbers*, respectively) no matter what. Or else… no dice.

Because Walmart doesn't meet any of the standards mentioned above, we must take a pass on it as an investment. Now, that does not mean that you have to stop *shopping* at Walmart. From a consumer standpoint, Wally World is probably the best retailer around. But from an *investing* standpoint, it's a no-go.

Now that you have been baptized in the enlightening waters of the value investing paradigm, you now understand that you must limit your investment options only to those companies that pass our stringent criteria inspection.

And WMT doesn't even come close.

So, ladies and gents, now that you know *where* to find the 12 criteria standards, by using our free, online resources, next on the list is teaching you how to open a brokerage account, so that you can actually begin investing in the stock market.

Vamanos, amigos…

CHAPTER 8

THE BROKERAGE ACCOUNT!

An online brokerage account is necessary in order to trade (in other words, buy and sell) stocks on the stock market.

There are tons of online brokerage companies. Some of the popular ones are: Etrade, TD Ameritrade, Ally, Charles Schwab, Fidelity, Merrill Edge, and Scottrade. These firms offer investors access to trading platforms, which are located on their online websites. Once you're done opening a brokerage account with one of these firms, you are allowed to use their trading platforms in order to buy and sell stocks on the web.

Seeing as there are so many online brokerage firms, how in the hell do I know which one to pick for my investment needs? you may be wondering.

The answer to that question is based on two things: savings and convenience.

Let's talk, first, about how to pick an online brokerage firm that will help you maximize your savings as you invest your way to your one-millionaire-dollar goal.

SAVINGS

Online brokerage firms make money by charging you a commission on each trade you make using their trading platforms. So, for example, at the time of this writing, Etrade.com's commission fee for a standard stock trade is $6.95. So every time I buy or sell shares using the Etrade platform, I have to pay $6.95 per transaction.

So, let's say I buy 10 shares of XYZ Company at $10 per share, using the Etrade investing platform. The cost of buying those shares would be $100 (10 shares x $10 = $100). But I'm not done yet. Because now I have to pay Etrade their commission fee of $6.95 for facilitating the transaction. Therefore, the final invoice would actually be $106.95 ($100.00 stock purchase + 6.95 Etrade commission fee = $106.95 final charge).

So, before picking your online broker, you want to do some research to find out which online brokerage firms are offering the lowest commission fees. Because the lower the commission fee, the more money you get to keep in your pocket—and thus, the more money you get to *save.*

But there is a kicker.

You shouldn't pick an online broker *solely* because their commission costs are low.

I know, I know. Sounds like I'm contradicting myself. First I tell you to search high and low for low-cost brokers. Then I tell you the opposite.

Sorry for the confusion.

But let me explain.

Some online brokers have not-so-cheap commission costs due to the breadth of their trading platforms. Meaning, their trading platforms contain a fountain of pertinent, detailed information, as well as up-to-date investing tools (such as comprehensive charts and stock screeners) that make it easier for their users to make well-timed and educated decisions. Which results in... (you got it) ... big-time profits.

In which case, paying a few cents (or even a few dollars) more in commission costs is well worth it. Why? Well, because in the investing world, having access to pertinent information can mean a world of a difference. (Like the difference between making a killing, or losing your shirt).

So, before you pick your broker, do some research online to see which firms out there are truly giving you the best bang for your buck. And by that I mean, you should search relentlessly for a broker that is going to give you both access to the most up-to-date information and investing tools, while also charging a reasonable commission fee that is commensurate with the service that they are providing.

Got it?

Good!

Now, let's talk about the role *convenience* plays when choosing an online broker. We will focus on two points: money transfers and stock screeners.

CONVIENCE

Money Transfers

After you open an online brokerage account (which I will show you how to do in a bit), the next step is to fund the account. Which means that you must transfer cash from your personal checking or savings account, into your online brokerage account. The transfer process sometimes takes a few days (and that's business—not calendar—days, at that). Which means that if you request a funds transfer from your personal bank on, let's say, Friday morning, the cash may not *actually* reach your brokerage account until Tuesday or Wednesday of the following week; sometimes maybe even Thursday of the ensuing week. And this, to some degree, limits your capacity to buy stocks at the drop of a hat (especially if your online brokerage account is not prematurely or adequately funded).

When I first started buying stocks, my online brokerage account was serviced by Etrade.com, while my personal checking account was held with Bank of America. So, whenever I wanted to buy a stock, I had to request a funds transfer from Bank of America (via the Etrade platform). Then I'd have to wait several days for the money to get wired from my Bank of America checking account to my Etrade trading account. I remember missing out on a few—not many—buying opportunities, due to the wait time associated with the money transfer.

Sometime after I started trading stocks, Bank of America (BOA) acquired Merrill Lynch, which was, at that time, the country's largest retail brokerage firm. Merrill Lynch had an online trading platform called Merrill Edge. Consequently, BOA's Merrill Lynch acquisition gave BOA customers access to the Merrill Edge trading platform. Which meant that BOA customers could now merge their personal checking/savings accounts with their stock market accounts. As a result, BOA customers could transfer money seamlessly between their personal and stock market accounts, whenever they chose, without having to wait days for a money transfer to go through. And this, invariably, improved a trader's reaction time.

(And we all know, in the world of finance, that time is money).

So, if you're going to be serious about trading stocks, it might be a good idea to open a checking and/or savings account with a retail bank that offers its customers a built-in, online brokerage service. That way you can merge your accounts, and eliminate the wait-time associated with transferring money from one banking institution to another.

Stock Screeners

Stock screeners are very important to a budding value investor like yourself. A stock screener is an investment tool, provided by some online brokerage firms, which helps a trader filter stocks, based on user-defined metrics.

So, for example, one of the twelve criteria we discussed in the previous chapter was the dividend criteria (which was criteria #2). And that criteria states that you should never buy a stock, unless it possesses a dividend payment of 2.5% or more. So, instead of manually going through a list containing the thousands and thousands of companies trading on the market, in search of those companies that shell out a 2.5% dividend, some trading platforms have stock screeners that allow you to input the information you are looking for (in our case, 2.5% dividend stocks), and then the stock screener will glean the entire market in search of all the stocks that meet your criteria.

Without you having to lift a *single* finger.

How fucking awesome is that, huh?

You must, by now, realize how extremely important (and convenient) a stock-screener tool is to your investment strategy. Because as a newly-christened, analytical stock picker, you are no longer content with investing in any old company, for the hell of it. You now understand that you should *only* be investing in fundamentally-sound companies. And a company can only be fundamentally-sound if it meets our 12 criteria (which we discussed at length in the previous two chapters).

So, having said that, it only behooves you to find an online trading platform that offers advanced stock-screening options. That way you can type all of the requisite criteria into the stock screener, and let the screener itself do all of the heavy lifting. The screener will then sift through the many companies trading on the market, until it finds the few companies that meet all (or a majority) of your 12 criteria.

That way, the only thing you have to do is wake up every morning, log into your online brokerage account, and check your stock-screener to see if it has found you any diamonds in the rough.

All of which will take you less than five minutes.

Now, how fucking convenient is that?

So, now that you know *what* to look for when picking an online brokerage firm—first, a reasonable commission fee structure that saves you money; second, a retail bank that offers a built-in trading platform so you can transfer money seamlessly from your personal checking/savings accounts to your market-trading account, without any wait-time; and third, an online trading platform that provides you with comprehensive stock screening options, so that you can quickly find the few companies that match all (or most) of your 12 criteria—let's now explore the steps needed to actually open and fund an online brokerage account.

For the sake of this example, I am going to show you how to open a Merrill Edge brokerage account. I am going to use Merrill Edge as an example because it is the one that I use. Merrill Edge is the built-in trading platform offered by my personal bank, Bank of America. Hence, I can merge all of my financial accounts (both personal and trading accounts) in order to more fluidly transfer money between them. Moreover, Merrill Edge provides me with all-inclusive stock-screening options that allow me to quickly glean the entire market in search of companies that meet my 12-criteria checklist.

So, ladies and gents, are you ready to open your very first online brokerage account?

Great!

Let's do it!

OPENING YOUR TRADING ACCOUNT

Let me start out by saying that you don't necessarily *need* a Bank of America checking/saving account in order to open a Merrill Edge investment account. I'm merely using Merrill Edge as an example because it is the trading platform that I currently use.

And let me also add that, while the steps for opening a Merrill Edge trading account may not be spot-on-the-same as the steps for opening, let's say, an Etrade trading account, the process is very similar. So if you successfully learn (or know) how to open an online account with one broker, the procedure is pretty much the same for opening accounts with other online brokerage firms.

So, let me take you through the steps:

Step 1: Open your online browser and type *www.merrilledge.com* in the address bar.

Step 2: Click on the "Open An Account" link on the top right-hand corner of the page.

Step 3: As of this writing, a screen with the following links will appear: "General Investing," "Retirement," "College Planning," "Merrill Edge Guided Investing," "Invest With An Advisor," "Small Business Account." Click on the "General Investing" link.

Step 4: Clicking on the "General Investing" link will produce two other drop-down options: "Online brokerage account" and "Trust & estate account." Click on the "Open Now" box/link that is under the "Online brokerage account" option.

Step 5: A pop-up screen will appear with the following options: "Individual Cash Management Account," "Joint Cash Management Account," and "Custodial Cash Management Account." Click on the clear bubble next to the "Individual Cash Management Account" option. Then click on the "Open Now" box/link that is at the bottom of the pop-up screen.

Step 6: Another screen entitled "What You'll Need" will appear. This screen merely tells you the information you'll need to complete the account registration process. As of this writing, some of the requisites listed on the page are: "Social security number and date of birth," "A valid mailing and email addresses," "Employment information," and "General financial information." Click on the blue link that reads "Continue," which is located at the bottom of the screen.

Step 7: Next, the screen will drop down, and you will see a section labeled, "Are you an existing client?" Beneath this section, there will be 3 choices: "I Have a Merrill Lynch User ID and Password," "I have Bank of America Online ID and Passcode for a personal account," and "I'm a new client. I don't have either one." If you have a Merrill Lynch account, click on the bubble next to the "I Have a Merrill Lynch User ID and Password" option. If you already have a Bank of America online account, click on the bubble next to the "I have Bank of America Online ID and Passcode for a personal account" option. And lastly, if you don't have either a Merrill Lynch account, or a Bank of America account, click on the bubble next to the "I'm a new client. I don't have either one" option. For the purposes of this example, let's click on the third option: "I'm a new client. I don't have either one."

Step 8: Next, a blue-boxed link will appear that reads: "Begin Application." Click on that link.

Step 9: Next, a screen titled "Primary applicant" will appear. On this screen, you will be asked to fill out "Personal Information." Fill out all of the relevant information, then click the "Continue" link at the bottom of the page.

Step 10: Next, the screen titled "Primary applicant" will appear again. But on this screen, you will be asked to fill out "Employment and financial information." Fill out all of the relevant information, then click the "Continue" link at the bottom of the page.

Step 11: Next, a screen titled "Account details" will appear. On this screen, you will be asked to fill out your preferred "Account features." You will be given 3 options: "Margin," "Deferred Debit Card," and "Check writing." Mainly, these options are different ways you can use/access the cash in your trading account. If you are a beginning trader, I would stay away from the "Margin" option; trading on margin is better suited for expert/experienced traders. Honestly, if you are trying to trade and save your way up to $1 million, it is probably unwise to give yourself any access to the cash that will be accumulating in the account. By cutting all physical access to the cash, you will be less tempted to withdraw funds from the account. So, for now, I would refrain from clicking on any of the options, and merely click the "Continue" link at the bottom of the page.

Step 12: Next, the screen titled "Account details" will appear again. But on this version of the screen, you will be asked to choose an "ID and Password," so that you can access your online account. Fill out all of the relevant information, then click the "Continue" link at the bottom of the page.

Step 13: Next, a screen titled "Review and submit your application" will appear. On this screen, you will be asked to fill out "Personal Information." Review all of the information on the page and make sure that it is accurate. When you're done doing that, click the "Continue to terms and conditions" link at the bottom of the page.

Step 14: Next, a screen titled "Terms & conditions (page 1 of 3)" will appear. On this screen, you will be asked to review the "Electronics communications disclosure." Review all of the information on the page. When you're finished, click on the checkbox at the bottom of the disclosure statement; this confirms that you agree with the company's disclosure agreement. Afterwards, click on the "Continue to next agreement" link at the bottom of the page.

Step 15: Next, a screen titled "Terms & conditions (page 2 of 3)" will appear. On this screen, you will be asked to review the "Tax certification form." Review all of the information on the page. When you're finished, click on the checkbox at the bottom of the tax form statement; this confirms that you agree with the company's tax disclosure agreement. Afterwards, click on the "Continue to final agreement" link at the bottom of the page.

Step 16: Next, a screen titled "Terms & conditions (page 3 of 3)" will appear. On this screen, you will be asked to review important account disclosures, privacy and affiliate marketing notices, and account attestations. Review all of the information on the page. When you're finished, click on the checkbox at the bottom of the disclosure statement; this confirms that you agree with the company's disclosure agreement. Afterwards, click on the "Submit application" link at the bottom of the page.

And *voila*! There you have it! You now have an official online brokerage account. And you should feel *damn* proud of yourself!

To fund your account, follow the remaining online instructions provided by Merrill Edge. Once you're done transferring the funds from your personal banking account into your brokerage account, you'll be all set to start buying and selling stocks.

Now, I will show you how to use the stock screener on your new trading platform to automatically find stocks that meet our investment standards. That way you don't have to spend countless hours manually searching for these individual stocks out of the thousands of stocks currently in existence on the market. All you'll have to do, each day you wake up, is log into your trading account, click on your stock screener (which will already be preset with all of the necessary criterion), and check to see if the screener has found any stocks for you that are worth investing in.

Remember, our criteria are extremely stringent, so rarely will the screener find a stock that meets them all. But be patient. Don't forget that we are literally searching for the near-perfect company to invest in; so, it's gonna take time. But when we do find it (meaning, when that company finally *does* show up on your stock screener), you can rest assured that the money you invest in it will be safe and sound.

Alrighty then. Let's go head and preset your stock screener.

PRE-SETTING YOUR STOCK SCREENER

In the previous section, I showed you how to open an online trading account using Merrill Edge. Now I will show you how to preset your stock screener using the same online broker.

We will program the stock screener to find stocks that meet the following criteria:

(1) PE Ratio between 0 and 15,
(2) Price/Book ratio between 0.6 and 2,
(3) Price/Book ratio between 0.6 and 2,
(4) Debt to Equity Ratio between 0 and 50%,
(5) Dividend Yield equal to or above 2.5%,
(6) Net Profit Margin equal to or above 10%,
(7) Return on Invested Capital equal to or above 10%,

(8) Return on Equity equal to or above 10%,
(9) Quick Ratio equal to or above 1.5,
(10) Current Ratio equal to or above 1.5,

If you look closely at the list above, you will notice that 2 criteria from our original 12 are missing. They are the True Value and Trend Numbers criteria.

Let me explain why this is.

Both the True Value and Trend Numbers criteria are functions that you will have to perform manually. The stock screener we are using will not be able to calculate these functions for you. If you need a refresher, go back to *Chapter 7: The Resources,* and re-read the True Value and Trend Numbers sections to reacquaint yourself with these criteria, including where to find them. As a reminder, you'll need to use the Marketwatch.com website to find the True Value number, and the Morningstar.com website to chart the company's Trend Numbers.

So—and this is very important, so listen up—if a stock appears on your stock screener, that does not mean that you automatically invest in it. You'll have to use the Marketwatch.com and Morningstar.com websites to make sure that the stock also meets the True Value and Trend Numbers requirements. And—I can't stress this enough—if a stock does not meet **both** the true value *and* trend numbers standards, you must **not** invest in it. Even if it meets all of the other ten criteria. What you *would* do at this point is keep the stock on your radar, and check on it periodically. And if, or when, it does meet the true value and trend numbers benchmark, then you can invest in it.

Got it?

Good.

So, with no further ado, let me show you how to set up the presets for your stock screener:

Step 1: Open your online browser and type *www.merrilledge.com* in the address bar.

Step 2: The home page will appear. On the left side of the screen, you will see a "Secure Log in" section. Go ahead and enter your user ID and password. When you're done entering that information, press the "Log in" link located underneath the user ID and password boxes.

Step 3: A page entitled "Account holdings for" should appear. Above the page title, you will find other links. If you hover your mouse over these links, they will produce drop-down menus. As of this writing, the links featured on this page are: "Accounts," "Trade," "Research," "Products," "Guidance & Retirement," and "Help & Support." Hover your mouse over the "Research" link. A drop-down menu will appear with various categories. The categories are: "Markets," "Investment Research," "Screeners," "Investing Tools," "Research & Insights," "Investing Resources," and "Simplified Investing." Click on the "Stock Screener" link beneath the "Screeners" category.

Step 4: A new page will then appear. On this page, you will see two links: "Custom Screens" and "Predefined Screens." Click on the "Custom Screens" link.

Step 5: On the "Custom Screens" page you will see the title "New Screen." Under this title there will be an assortment of criterion to pick from. So, let's pick the ones we need.

1. **To Preset the Dividend Criteria**: Click on the "Dividend Yield" link. Click on the "Manual Entry" link. Click on the drop-down menu box and choose the "Greater than or equal to" link. In the box to the right, type: 2.5 (for the 2.5% threshold that we require). Click on the "Apply filters" link at the bottom of the screen. This will bring you back to the "Customs Screens" page, with your Dividend Yield preset cued up.
2. **To Preset the P/E Ratio Criteria**: Now click on the "P/E Ratio (TTM)" link under the "New Screen" title. Click on the "Manual Entry" link; click on the drop-down menu box and choose the "Less than or equal to" link. In the box to the right, type 15 (for the 15 or below threshold that our standards require). Click on the "Apply filters" link at the bottom of the screen. This will bring you back to the "Customs Screens" page, with your "P/E Ratio (TTM)" preset cued up.
3. **To Preset the P/B Ratio Criteria**: Now click on the "Advanced Criteria" link under the "New Screen" title. Under the section titled "Choose a filter," click on the "Valuation" link. A drop-down box will appear, click on the "Price/Book (MRQ)" link. Click on the

"Manual Entry" link that appears on the side screen. Click on the drop-down menu box and choose the "Range" link. In the "from" box, type: 0.6, and in the "to" box, type 1.5 (for the 0.6 – 1.5 threshold that our standards require). Then click on the "Apply filters" link at the bottom of the screen. This will bring you back to the "Customs Screens" page, with your "Price/Book (MRQ)" preset cued up.

4. **To Preset the P/S Ratio Criteria**: Now click on the "Advanced Criteria" link under the "New Screen" title. Under the section titled "Choose a filter," click on the "Valuation" link. A drop-down box will appear, click on the "Price/Sales (TTM)" link. Click on the "Manual Entry" link that appears on the side screen. Click on the drop-down menu box and choose the "Range" link. In the "from" box, type 0.6, and in the "to" box, type 1.5 (for the 0.6 – 1.5 threshold that our standards require). Then click on the "Apply filters" link at the bottom of the screen. This will bring you back to the "Customs Screens" page, with your "Price/Sales (TTM)" preset cued up.
5. **To Preset the D/E Ratio Criteria**: Now click on the "Advanced Criteria" link under the "New Screen" title. Under the section titled "Choose a filter," click on the "Financial Strength" link. A drop-down box will appear, click on the "Debt to Equity (MRQ)" link. Click on the "Manual Entry" link that appears on the side screen. Click on the drop-down menu box and choose the "Less than or equal to" link. In the box to the right, type: 50 (for the 50% or below threshold that our standards require). Click on the "Apply filters" link at the bottom of the screen. This will bring you back to the "Customs Screens" page, with your "Debt to Equity (MRQ)" preset cued up.
6. **To Preset the Quick Ratio Criteria**: Now click on the "Advanced Criteria" link under the "New Screen" title. Under the section titled "Choose a filter," click on the "Financial Strength" link. A drop-down box will appear, click on the "Quick Ratio (MRQ)" link. Click on the "Manual Entry" link that appears on the side screen. Click on the drop-down menu box and choose the "Greater than or equal to" link. In the box to the right, type: 1.5 (for the 1.5 or higher

threshold that our standards require). Click on the "Apply filters" link at the bottom of the screen. This will bring you back to the "Customs Screens" page, with your "Quick Ratio (MRQ)" preset cued up.

7. **To Preset the Current Ratio Criteria**: Now click on the "Advanced Criteria" link under the "New Screen" title. Under the section titled "Choose a filter," click on the "Financial Strength" link. A drop-down box will appear, click on the "Current Ratio (MRQ)" link. Click on the "Manual Entry" link that appears on the side screen. Click on the drop-down menu box and choose the "Greater than or equal to" link. In the box to the right, type: 1.5 (for the 1.5 or higher threshold that our standards require). Click on the "Apply filters" link at the bottom of the screen. This will bring you back to the "Customs Screens" page, with your "Current Ratio (MRQ)" preset cued up.
8. **To Preset the Return On Equity Criteria**: Now click on the "Advanced Criteria" link under the "New Screen" title. Under the section titled "Choose a filter," click on the "Financial Strength" link. A drop-down box will appear, click on the "Return on Equity (TTM)" link. Click on the "Manual Entry" link that appears on the side screen. Click on the drop-down menu box and choose the "Greater than or equal to" link. In the box to the right, type: 10 (for the 10% or higher threshold that our standards require). Click on the "Apply filters" link at the bottom of the screen. This will bring you back to the "Customs Screens" page, with your "Return on Equity (TTM)" preset cued up.
9. **To Preset the Return On Invested Capital Criteria**: Now click on the "Advanced Criteria" link under the "New Screen" title. Under the section titled "Choose a filter," click on the "Financial Strength" link. A drop-down box will appear, click on the "Return on Invested Capital (TTM)" link. Click on the "Manual Entry" link that appears on the side screen. Click on the drop-down menu box and choose the "Greater than or equal to" link. In the box to the right, type: 10 (for the 10% or higher threshold that our standards require). Click on the "Apply filters" link at the bottom of the screen. This will bring you back to the "Customs Screens" page, with your "Return on Invested Capital (TTM)" preset cued up.

10. To Preset the Profit Margin Criteria: Now click on the "Advanced Criteria" link under the "New Screen" title. Under the section titled "Choose a filter," click on the "Financial Strength" link. A drop-down box will appear, click on the "Profit Margin (TTM)" link. Click on the "Manual Entry" link that appears on the side screen. Click on the drop-down menu box and choose the "Greater than or equal to" link. In the box to the right, type: 10 (for the 10% or higher threshold that our standards require). Click on the "Apply filters" link at the bottom of the screen. This will bring you back to the "Customs Screens" page, with your "Profit Margin (TTM)" preset cued up.
11. To Save Your Stock Screening Criteria: You should now be on the "Customs Screens" page. Under the "Customs Screen" link, you will see the title "New Screen." And next to that title, you will see a link that reads, "Save this screen." Click on the "Save this screen" link. A message box entitled "Save Screen Criteria" will pop up, allowing you to save this group of criteria so that you can easily access them later. Type whatever name you want, then click on the "Save Screen" link underneath.
12. To Access Your Stock Screening Criteria: You should again be on the "Customs Screens" page. To access your saved screener, simply click on the tiny "Saved Screens" link on the right side of the page. Then click on the link with the saved name that you chose. This is the stock-screener page you will check on a regular basis, to see if the screener has found any stocks on your behalf that are worth investing in.

CHAPTER RECAP

And that, ladies and gentlemen, is how you set up your stock screener. You are now officially ready to trade securities. Every morning (or week, or month, the choice is yours), wake up and check your stock screener. If a company's stock shows up on your screener, it means that the stock has automatically met 10 out of our 12 criteria. Thus, the stock is worth further investigation.

What you'll need to do then, to determine whether or not the stock is worth actually investing in, is check to see if the stock meets the other two criteria. That is to say, the stock must also be selling at a discount to its true value, and the stock's trend numbers must be stable, or rising, dating back ten years or so. The stock must meet these final two criteria, or else it is not in play.

At least, not for you.

Again, seldom will you find a stock that meets all of our criteria. This is where your patience comes into play. Patience is a successful stock picker's most valuable asset. Don't believe me? Well then, let's ask the man himself.

Us: Hey, Warren, buddy. Is patience a crucial skillset needed to successfully pick stocks?

Warren Buffett: "You do things when the opportunities come along. I've had periods in my life when I've had a bundle of ideas come along, and I've [also] had long dry spells.[23] Successful investing takes time."[24]

Okay, so there you have it.

Now you know how to open an online brokerage account, as well as set up your stock screener. You've also learned the necessary criteria for picking a stock. So, let's move on to the next chapter, where I will show you the circumstances under which you should sell your stocks, in order to make a tidy profit.

[23] https://medium.com/luchini-thoughts/warren-buffetts-greatest-skill-is-patience-10c0a861ee8f
[24]http://www.fool.com/investing/general/2014/09/28/25-best-warren-buffett-quotes.aspx

CHAPTER 9

THE SELL!

No one—not even Warren Buffett—keeps the same stocks forever.

There comes a point in time when you must sell the stocks you've bought, no matter how much you cherish them. In this chapter we will discuss when it is the right time to sell.

There are only two reasons why you should sell a stock. First, if the stock becomes way overpriced. And second, if there is a change in the company's fundamental economics—which usually occurs following either a change in leadership, or a change in the company's competitive landscape.

Let's discuss each sell-impetus individually.

THE STOCK IS OVERPRICED

Warren's most famous quote is about... (well, you guessed it) ... money. And he has this to say: "Rule #1: Never lose money. Rule #2: Never forget rule #1."

Your money is sacred. It is—for all intents and purposes—your life source. Without it—actually speaking—you cannot live. (At least not for long, not in this world). But with an abundance of it, you can live life beyond your wildest dreams.

Money is important.

No. Money is *paramount.*

And that's why you should never lose it.

When you buy a stock at a discount price and it goes up, you make a profit. At least on paper. In order to turn those paper profits (which the industry calls *unrealized gains*), into *actual* cold, hard cash (which the industry dubs *realized gains*), you must actually *sell* the stock on the stock market.

But this is easier said than done. Especially when greed starts to settle in. Let me explain.

Say for example, an investor buys a stock that is worth $1.25 for, say, $1.00 (which means that said investor bought the stock at a discount to true value—which is *great!*). Then, the market does its thing, and the stock begins to creep up. $1.50. $1.75. $2.00. And the investor thinks, *oh my god, this stock really fucking rocks.* He/she forgets immediately that the stock is only worth $1.25. Instead, they are blinded by greed. All they see is that ticker going up, and up, and up. $2.25. $2.50. *Holy fucking shit,* they think. *I'm freaking rich.*

But, actually, they're not.

Rich, that is.

On *paper* they have achieved unrealized profits of $1.50 per share. On *paper* they have earned a profit of 150% (which is fucking awesome). But in *actuality,* they have not made a single dime. And they *won't* make a dime... until they sell the shares on the open market, thereby turning their *unrealized* gains into *realized* cash.

But, out of greed, they don't do that. Instead, they clamp down on that overpriced stock as if they were newborn babies, and the stock was their mother's tit. They nestle close to it, checking the ticker every day, every hour, every second, even.

And then, as is always the case, an event occurs (or doesn't occur—you never know with Mr. Market), and the stock begins to go down. From $2.50 to $2.25. Then $2.10. Then $2.00. Uh-oh. The Feds just hiked up interest rates. *Bam!* The stock gets hammered again. Uh-oh, there was a tornado in Japan. *Wham!* The stock gets clipped once more. Now the stock is down to $1.10. But that investor keeps sucking on the tit. Refusing to let it go, despite how sour the milk has become. They are still blinded by greed. They still remember when the stock had gone up to $2.50. And they think, *maybe it will go back up again. Just maybe.*

But maybe never happens.

And before they can blink twice, news of war in the middle east (an event that has nothing to do with the actual company's stock, itself) causes the country to go ape-shit, thereby forcing stock investors to unload even more shares, bringing the stock's price down to a mind-numbing $0.75 per share. And guess what? Compelled by fear, and smitten by the market panic, the investor sells the stock.

At a *loss* (a $0.25 per share loss, since they originally bought the stock at $1.00).

And not just a paper loss, either. This time it's a real, fucking loss.

The above scenario is all too common. And as a stock picker, you will invariably find yourself in a similar situation. But *you* will never make the same mistake. Why is that? Because you're not just any kind of investor. You are a *value* investor. And value investors—like our main man, Warren Buffett—always remember the two most important rules about investing: Rule #1: Never lose money. Rule #2: Never forget rule #1.

When you purchase a stock at a discount to its true value, and the market re-prices that stock at a valuation that surpasses its true value, it's time to think about selling the stock. Because in the long—or short—run, Mr. Market *will* realize that he's made a mistake, and he will not hesitate to price the stock back down to true value, or lower.

That's why it's crucial to strike while the iron's hot.

Take your profits and run. Run, Forest. Run like the wind, goddamnit!

But, of course, every rule has an exception. And the exception to taking profits and running with them is that, if you are able to purchase stock in a wonderful, wonderful company, that is to say, a company that is number one—or number two—in its field due to some competitive advantage it possesses over its rivals, then it may be a good idea to hold on to such a stock, even after substantial paper profits have been made. *Why is that?* you ask. Well, companies with durable competitive advantages are so hard to find, that when you do have an opportunity to purchase their stocks, you should do so, with the purpose of holding onto those shares for the long-term.

Let's use Warren Buffett as an example.

At present, Warren Buffett has about 46 publicly-traded stocks in his stock market portfolio (which is a highly concentrated portfolio by any standards, let alone for an investor with billions and billions in capital to invest).[25] But out of

[25] http://www.cnbc.com/berkshire-hathaway-portfolio/

those 46 stocks, there are four stocks which Warren Buffett calls his "Big 4." And while he is apt to sell shares of the other 42 stocks, Buffett rarely, if ever, sells shares of his "Big 4" stocks. Warren Buffett's Big 4 stocks are: Coca-Cola (which Warren began buying in 1987), Wells Fargo (which Warren has owned since 1989), American Express (which Warren began acquiring in 1964), and IBM (which Warren began purchasing in 2011). These four companies account for $71.9 billion of the $161.9 billion in Buffett's portfolio, in terms of holding value. That means that a staggering 44% of Buffett's entire caboodle—with regards to his public portfolio—is vested in just four stocks. And that's been the case, for ages.

Thus, two questions come to mind. The first question is: How is it that Warren Buffett is comfortable with investing almost half of his money in just four stocks? And the second question is: Why does Buffett rarely—if ever—sell any shares of those four stocks?

The answer to both questions can be summed up with three words: Durable competitive advantage.

While Warren has bought and sold shares of many companies during his tenure as the world's most successful stock picker, he is very hesitant to sell shares of the Big 4, primarily because Coca-Cola, Wells Fargo, American Express, and IBM have competitive advantages that put them a step ahead of all their rivals (though, Warren Buffett *did* sell shares of his IBM stock in May of 2017, due to changes in IBM's competitive landscape—a matter we will discuss a bit later in this chapter).

So, let's do a quick recap. When you buy a stock at a discount to its true value, if the market price rises above that true value, consider selling the stock and taking your profits. That is the best way to guard against monetary loss. Because, when you don't take your profits and run, you become like a greedy speculator. Which means that you have forsaken your fundamental, value-investing roots, and have become like the rest of the market heretics, a bunch of prospectors mining mindlessly for usurious profits.

So, keep this in mind: Always base your selling decisions on fundamental facts (like a stock becoming overpriced), instead of greed. And the only time you *shouldn't* sell an overpriced stock is if you own stock in a company that has a durable competitive advantage over its rivals, thereby making that company's stock an ideal long-term play.

Got it?

Cool.

Let's discuss the second reason you should sell: when there is a change in a company's fundamental economics.

CHANGE IN THE COMPANY'S FUNDAMENTAL ECONOMICS

When a company's trend numbers begin to decline or waiver, you should start to worry.

We discussed the trend numbers at length in chapters six sand seven. But just as a reminder, the trend numbers are: sales, earnings per share, book value per share, free cash flow, and working capital.

These numbers will usually start to waiver following two major events. Firstly, when there is a change in leadership at the company, for the worst. Or secondly, when there is a change in the competitive landscape in which the company is operating.

CHANGE IN LEADERSHIP

Most start-up companies—and companies in general—fail. But there are a select few that do make it. And they don't just make it; they make it *big!* And many times, the company's success has more to do with its leaders, than the actual product or service the company is providing.

A great leader is a visionary. He/she is someone who instills confidence in his troops. He/she is transparent, and operates with stalwart integrity. He/she is selfless, and always puts the needs of the company first. A great leader is also a tireless innovator who performs his/her job responsibilities not because they are getting paid to do so, but rather, because it is their *calling* in life. Such leaders are so passionate about what they do, they'd probably do it for free.

There are a few founders/CEO's that fit the above bill. Men and women who have turned fledgling start-ups or takeover acquisitions into successful behemoths. Bill Gates (of Microsoft), Jeff Bezos (of Amazon), and Oprah Winfrey (of Harpo Productions) are a few names that come to mind. And so does our guy, Warren Buffett. Although Buffett's company, Berkshire Hathaway, was not a start-up when he took it over, it *was* a dying textile mill that was experiencing losses in the millions every year. Whereas now, it is the world's preeminent holding company, achieving net profits of $24 billion +

annually, while owning a variety of successful subsidiaries in different market sectors, from Dairy Queen, to Benjamin Moore, to Geico.

And it's all due to Warren Buffett and Charlie Munger, Berkshire Hathaway's CEO and vice-chairman, respectively. Without their vision, Berkshire Hathaway, the company, might not even exist today.

So if a company meets all of our criteria and proves to be fundamentally strong (economically speaking), that company's stock may be worth purchasing. But, as you continue to own the stock, keep an eye out for changes in management. Why? Well, because management might've been the reason why the company was successful in the first place. So if the management goes, so too might the company's profits.

Think of a good company as a champion thoroughbred. No matter what the horse's pedigree, on its own the animal can't even find its way to the track, let alone win a race. But with a good jockey guiding its every step, the horse can compete and win, earning its owners tons of money.

A thorough analysis of a company's management is necessary in order to make a wise investment decision. So keep your eyes on the jockeys. Because if that horse begins to underperform (meaning, if those trend numbers start heading south), it may have nothing to do with the horse, and everything to do with the guy/gal cracking the whip.

Either way, it may be time to pull your profits and run.

CHANGE IN COMPETITIVE LANDSCAPE

But, sometimes, it's not the jockey, and it truly *is* the horse.

A thoroughbred at the height of his career is not the same as a thoroughbred in the twilight of his career. Perhaps, in its prime, the horse was unbeatable, due to its superior strength, grace, speed, and fine genetic pedigree. But as time passed, the horse got older, fatter, and slower. While the other pure-bloods around him seemed to get younger, leaner, faster, and bolder.

As the old saying goes: "Father Time is undefeated." So when that horse—despite its fine pedigree—passes its prime, it doesn't matter what jockey you strap to his saddle. The horse simply won't be able to measure up to the other purebreds. Because his *time* is over.

If you invest in a company, and you notice—perhaps years later—that their trend numbers begin to waiver, if there hasn't been any significant changes in management, look immediately to that company's competitive playing field. Chances are, other leaner, meaner, bolder players have entered the playing field, and have declared war on your aging thoroughbred-company.

And while the courageous thing might be to hang tough and let your investment prove to you that it is battle-tested and impervious to defeat, the reality of the matter might simply be that there are other companies out there who can offer better services or products at better prices than the company you invested in. Thus, placing your company on the road to antiquity.

At which point, it's time to get the fuck outta that investment.

Don't believe me?

Well, let's see what Warren Buffet did when faced with the same dilemma.

As you already know, IBM is one of Warren's "Big 4" holdings (the others being Coca-Cola, Wells Fargo, and American Express). Warren Buffett is famously known for *increasing* his positions in the Big 4 over the years, while hesitating to sell a single share of the Big 4, due to his staunch faith in the durable competitive advantages they possessed in their respective market sectors.

So when the market got wind—in the first two quarters of 2017—that Warren Buffett had sold a third of his IBM shares, everyone was downright perplexed. *Why, oh why, Warren are you selling your IBM stocks?* everyone wanted to know. After all, IBM *is* a giant in the tech space. A $144 billion behemoth with long-standing credibility (shit, they've been around since 1911 for Christ sake, outflanking one competitor after the other).

But this is what Warren Buffett had to say during a CNBC interview, following the sale of his IBM shares: "I don't value IBM the same way that I did six years ago when I started buying... I've revalued it somewhat downward... IBM is a big strong company. But they've got big strong competitors, too."[26]

And can you guess what Warren Buffett did next?

He bought Apple, Inc. stock.

That's right.

Buffett bought IBM's "big strong" competitor in the tech space. And Warren didn't acquire a mere pittance, either. He fucking went to town, scooping up an astounding 2.6% of Apple's outstanding shares by March of 2017 (the same period when he was unloading IBM stock).

[26] http://fortune.com/2017/05/04/warren-buffett-ibm-berkshire-hathaway/

So, what lesson can we glean from Warren's actions? Well, first and foremost, a stock's valuation matters when it comes to making investment decisions. (Warren Buffett: "I don't *value* IBM the same way I did six years ago…"). And secondly, when a company is besieged by significant competition—no matter what that company's accomplishments in the past—it may be time to pull out of it as an investment. Because nothing hurts profits like competition. (Warren Buffett: "IBM is a big strong company. But they've got big strong *competitors*, too.").

And, just so you know, IBM's trend numbers were on a steady decline in all categories: Sales, Earnings per share, Book value per share, Free cash flow, *and* Working capital. While Apple's trend numbers in the same period were flourishing. A fact which, I'm sure, was not lost on Warren Buffett.

Chapter Recap

So, ladies and gents, there you have it.

Never forget that—when it comes to investing in stocks—you are not a business *owner.* You are an allocator of capital. Meaning, your sole job is to allocate money where it will grow exponentially, as quickly as possible. Your allegiance is to your profit margin, not to a brick-and-mortar operation. So, when you find a good stock that meets a majority of our value-investing criteria, dive in. But if, over time, your investment's fundamental strengths begin to wane—due to a change in leadership, or increased competition—do not hesitate to sell. And, if you can help it, sell while there's still a profit to be made.

And not a second later.

Or else you will regret it for the rest of your life.

Capisce?

Great!

So, let's head into the championship rounds (Chapters 10 and 11), where we will discuss the importance of execution (because without it, your reading this book will have been all for naught), followed by a few disclaimers (because, after all, I'm no fortune-teller, people).

CHAPTER 10

THE EXECUTION!

This is going to be the shortest chapter in the book. I promise.

There are two kinds of people in this world: those who watch; and those who do. When you're done reading this book, you're gonna have to make what will probably be the biggest decision of your life.

Are you going to continue to watch others become millionaires (an astounding 1,700 Americans are becoming millionaires every day)?27

Or are you going to do what it takes to become one yourself?

The blueprint is in this book. But let's be honest. Half of you are going to put this book down and forget about everything you've just read. Then, a few days later, you'll start bitching and complaining again about how miserable your life is, and you'll start praying and wishing for a better one, the desire for financial independence eating away at your very soul.

But that's as far as you'll ever get: praying and wishing (and bitching and complaining).

[27] http://fortune.com/2016/11/22/us-millionaire-wealth-inequality/

And then there's the other half of you readers who will not put this book down. You'll keep it close. And you'll crack it open from time to time, to refresh your memory, as you begin to implement the necessary steps to become a stock market millionaire. You'll save your money. You'll budget your expenses. You'll open up a brokerage account. And you'll start investing your savings in stocks that meet our value investing criteria. And you'll reinvest all of your profits until, one day, you go to open your brokerage account, and find one million dollars chillin' in your portfolio.

And then you'll close your eyes, and let the tears stream down your cheeks. Because in that moment you'll know that the life you've always wanted to live has now arrived.

So, I ask you now: Which category of reader will you be?

(See, I told you this chapter would be short!)

CHAPTER 11

THE DISCLAIMERS!

We've reached the final chapter of the book. *At last.* So, as you get ready to implement the strategies outlined in the pages of this volume, I want you to keep a few things in mind. I'm not here to bullshit you. I'm here, rather, to empower you with knowledge. I'm here, dear reader, to keep it real.

So, in the spirit of keeping it real, here are a few disclaimers that you should keep in mind:

Disclaimer #1: This book doesn't promise to turn you into a millionaire. No. What this book does do is map out, in detail, the strategies used by the greatest investor of all time to build his fortune. Beginning with his savings and budgeting habits, and ending with his value-oriented investment tactics.

Disclaimer #2: There is an inherent risk of loss that comes with every form of investment. Even investments in the stock market. Heck, especially investments in the stock market (just ask everyone who lost their shirts in the Great Depression of 1929, or in the Great Recession of 2008). No one knows what tomorrow will bring. A business you've invested in can be thriving one minute, then file for bankruptcy the next, taking your entire cash caboodle down with it. What this book does is give you strategies to minimize the risk of loss when investing in companies on the stock market.

Disclaimer #3: Fortunes are made when there is blood on the streets. Meaning, you have to have the patience to wait for a market crash or downturn; and then you have to have the balls to invest in companies (good companies) when they're prices are at rock bottom levels because the rest of the market is pulling their money out of them. It's practically the only way you are going to be able to turn your $46,800 in savings into $1 million in less than nine years. Bull markets are not good for your portfolio. Market crashes, on the other hand… we love those. Take it from the man himself, Warren Buffett: "Be fearful when others are greedy; and be greedy when others are fearful."

Enough said.

Disclaimer #4: If you don't begin implementing the steps I've outlined for you in this book right now, while they're still fresh in your mind, you'll never begin. Begin now, or never.

The choice is yours.

THE END

Cheat Sheet

12 Criteria	Formula	Resource
1-True Value (TV)	Total Equity/ Diluted Shares Outstanding	Marketwatch.com
2-Dividend = 2.5%+	Annual Dividends Per Share / Price Per Share	Marketwatch.com
3-ROIC = 10%+	Net Income (after tax) – Dividends/ Total Capital Invested	Marketwatch.com
4-ROE = 10%+	Net income (pre-tax & pre-dividends) / Shareholders' Equity	Marketwatch.com
5-Net Profit (NP) Margin = 10%+	Total Revenue – Total Expenses = Net Profit, and Net Profit/ Total Revenue = Net Profit Margin	Marketwatch.com
6-P/E Ratio = < 15%	Market price / Earnings Per Share	Marketwatch.com
7-Price/Sales Ratio = .6 - 1.5	Market Price / Sales Per Share	Marketwatch.com
8-Price/Book Ratio = .6 - 1.5	Market Price / Total Assets - (Intangible Assets + Liabilities)	Marketwatch.com
9-Debt/Equity Ratio (DE) = <.50	Total Liability / Shareholder Equity	Marketwatch.com
10-Current Ratio = 1.5+	Current Assets / Current Liabilities	Marketwatch.com
11-Quick Ratio = 1.5+	Current Assets (Including Inventory) / Current Liabilities	Marketwatch.com
12-Trend Numbers = Stable and/or Increasing	Steady and/or growing Sales, Earnings Per Share (EPS), Book Value per Share, Free Cash Flow, Working Capital	Morningstar.com (check over a ten-year period)

12 Criteria Rule

In order for a stock to be deemed worthy of purchase, it must meet at least 9 out of the 12 criteria listed above. Out of those 9 criteria, criteria #1 and #12 must ALWAYS be present. If BOTH criteria #1 and #12 are not present within the 9 criteria, the stock MUST NOT be purchased.

Determining A Stock's Net Worth (or True Value)

"Total Equity" divided by "Diluted Shares Outstanding"

Online Resources

- Marketwatch.com
- Morningstar.com

Online Brokerage Firms

- Merrilledge.com
- Etrade.com
- Scottrade.com
- TDameritrade.com
- Ally.com
- Charlesschwab.com
- Fidelity.com

NOTES

NOTES

NOTES

Letter to the Reader

I would like to thank all of the readers of this book for their kind purchase. I am heavily indebted to you, for it is you who makes this craft we authors call "writing" worthwhile. I hope you enjoyed reading *How Did Warren Buffett Succeed?* as much as I enjoyed writing it. If you liked the book, please spread the word by going to Amazon.com and writing a short review. I believe that personal finance and stock market investing are indispensable skills we must all strive to master. They can mean the difference between a comfortable (and early) retirement, or ensuing financial ruin. So please, apply the methods in this book to your daily life, and spread the message of sound, financial stewardship to your family and loved ones. Never forget, *Willful waste makes for woeful want.* Until next, dear reader.

James E. Pierre, JD

About the Author

James Pierre is also the author of *Gambino: The Rise*, a crime novel about the mafia. He is the founder of Hartford Holding Company, LLC, a family-owned and operated investment firm specializing in securities and real estate acquisitions. He lives in Connecticut with his wife, Katrina, a yoga enthusiast. Pierre has a Juris Doctorate degree from the University of Massachusetts School of Law. When he is not writing, he and his wife enjoy traveling to tropical islands. Pierre also loves to watch, and engage in, athletic competition, basketball, football, and (more recently) weight-lifting being his favorite sports.

Made in the USA
Monee, IL
04 November 2026

67377566R00095